HALFWAY TO ASPHODEL
2020 Omnibus Edition

VISHVARAJ CHAUHAN

HALFWAY TO ASPHODEL
2020 Omnibus Edition

Halfway To Asphodel
"If you don't speak, you're *halfway to asphodel* already."

(halfwaytoasphodel.com)

ALSO BY VISHVARAJ CHAUHAN

The Best of Halfway To Asphodel: 2015-2017 (First Edition of this book)

Elpis in a Jar

To all those who are waging a war within.

Sometimes you have to let things go to allow them to find you again.

Halfway To Asphodel: 2020 Omnibus Edition
(The Best of Halfway To Asphodel 2015-2017 Second Edition)
Author: Vishvaraj Chauhan

Editor: Self
Cover Design: Self
Halfway To Asphodel Logo: Deepal Bhavsar, Ahmedabad

Also available globally as an E-book.

ISBN: 978-9354076060

Imprint: Independently published.

The biggest fight is not the actual combat, it is the first step into the arena. It is the fist that raises first which is the most bold. It is the demand that is shouted first which is the most notable. Everything else, then, follows it's own course.

So here's to those who step up for for others. Who raise their hands to pull up and bring others up. Who use their words to raise their voice unequivocally for the right cause and in favour of the wronged. Here's to those who war to save others.

But I raise a cup to those who battle to save themselves. You deserve everything good you need.

Author's Note

I have always believed that greater proficiency in language has to be used to help others communicate, and put forward their points and ideas better rather than putting them off and unnecessarily flaunting. Because words, if properly woven can create a web of intricate detail which enchants you, traps you into a world with special abilities and special scenarios. They can be the ointment on the scars of life. Words, if carelessly used and spewed, can corrupt, harm, create strife and be the source of death. The pen is mightier than the sword, and the tongue is even greater. A drawn sword can still be sheathed, a blabbered insult cannot. Sometimes the deepest scars are not visible, and are a reason of inappropriately said unwanted words. While the usage of words is a delicate job, the lack of words is the workshop of illegitimate thoughts. So many differences and distances have popped up in lives all around the world simply because the parties haven't exchanged enough between them.

Words are not just permutations and combinations of the alphabet governed by a set of rules, they are a key. The key to yourself, to your communication partner, and to the entire world.

Such is this attempt, to pen my thoughts into words which have often served as the key for me to myself.

The inspiration for the name of the blog and the book, "Halfway To Asphodel" (halfwaytoasphodel.com) comes from a certain Rick Riordan, who in the final book of The Heroes Of Olympus Series, The Blood Of Olympus; wrote;

"'The main thing about ghosts – most of them have lost their voices. In Asphodel, millions of them wander around aimlessly, trying

to remember who they were. You know why they end up like that? Because in life they never took a stand one way or another. They never spoke out, so they were never heard. Your voice is your identity. If you don't use it,' he said with a shrug, 'you're ***halfway to Asphodel*** *already.'"*

That is a reference in Greek mythology, where the Fields of Asphodel were the place in the underworld (as the Greeks believed) where the people who did neither good nor bad went. They roamed around aimlessly there, searching for a purpose. Since I didn't want to be in the Fields of Asphodel, the name 'Halfway To Asphodel' gave me a constant reminder to write and keep writing, sharing my opinions so that I can call myself truly alive.

Halfway To Asphodel came into public view on April 8, 2015. The journey since has been akin to the first post which was published that day, '**A Journey on the Edge of the Door**.' The three years that followed are a testament to the graciousness of those who took the pain to read regularly the posts, criticise and encourage me, but most importantly, kept me going. Various weekly, monthly and an occasional annual prize came along, but the biggest satisfaction arrived when reviews echoed the sentiment of the post, or even better, claimed to have their hearts moved and feelings touched. Over this time, there have been innumerable moments of pride and happiness, and I cannot fathom how juiceless my life would be without Halfway To Asphodel.

The blog took over my monotone like nothing else had, and I began caring of it like a father. I loved it, nurtured it, and took pride in it as much as any parent, which gives me the opportunity to thank my parents for their support and love throughout my writing. Over these years, with countless nights fretting over the immediate and long term future of the blog made me appreciate the immense sacrifices and lost sleep my parents have endured for me. My love for Halfway To Asphodel made me appreciate my parents' love for me.

Furthermore, I would like to thank JP Rambling for being an absolutely phenomenal guide and mentor. Without his guidance and expertise which he passed on to me without any hesitation, I would not be the writer I am, or even more, the person I am. His tolerance, patience, wisdom and maturity are some of the traits I admire the most, and feel like incorporating into my being. I remain very grateful to him. He very graciously agreed to write the foreword to my second book, 'Elpis in a Jar", released in 2019.

Special thanks to Deepal Bhavsar for designing the logo of the blog.

This second edition of the first book, "The Best of Halfway To Asphodel: 2015-2017", includes my work from 2018 to 2020. Certain changes in titles of chapters are done, as 'Letters to Silence' is now reverted to their original name, "Letters to Celisen", Celisen being an anagram for silence.

Thank you for choosing this book. It consists of five sections - Contemplative Philosophy, Personal, Romance, Letters To Silence, and Poetry. In your hands, in front of your eyes rests a piece of my soul. It is the product of my sleepless nights and pleasant ecstasy. You have a piece of me. I hope you will enjoy it.

Contemplative Philosophy consists of articles that choose one topic and discuss it philosophically, in a way that is contemplated by my mind. Personal articles have a touch of intimacy and relation, which I hope you can relate to. Romance contains essays about my idea of love, it's associated despair and other feelings. Letters To Celisen are my letters addressed to silence. I have always perceived silence as a teacher and more, as you'll see. As mentioned abpve, initially posted as Letters To Celisen, readers had to guess who Celisen was. You already know who, or rather what it is. The Poetry section is my attempt at poems, which are often of the rhyming variety.

It has been a dream to write these.

You can find me on social media (Facebook, Twitter and Instagram) at @Funadrius.

Vishvaraj Chauhan

Halfway To Asphodel.com

CONTENTS

PERSONAL

ROMANCE

LETTERS TO CELISEN

POETRY

Halfway To Asphodel.com

CONTEMPLATIVE PHILOSOPHIES

A Journey On The Edge Of The Door

Time has its way of latching onto your deepest entrails, test them, and you either come out of it better or you don't. When it rains, it pours. Such was this past month, grinding, hilarious, and awfully real.

Negotiating after long term absence is always difficult, be it in relationships, work, studies or plain materialistic considerations. Sometimes the absence is sudden and permanent, which leaves you numb. You try to move on, to focus and work; and eventually, you do. But that nag remains. The work may drown you out, but the sleep will keep you afloat. Recreation may let you go, but eventually you come back, to a point where things feel incomplete, unjust and deflated.

I figure that life is a train journey - a typical Indian train journey in a packed general compartment. All kinds of people are there, each no doubt wanting to upgrade, in a reservation class. Isn't it the way in reality? No one is actually satisfied with what they have got, and whether should one be or not is debatable. You struggle in the train, to get in, to sustain. You fight your way through to the doors of life, fight to find your feet and hold your place. Normally you know where you want to go, yet every intermediate station entices you.

Because it's the unknown you love, you love it so much that it frightens you.

Maybe you know that you have no purpose on that station. Yet you're there, either to escort someone, or to patiently wait for your time.

For the unknown is your mistress, the known a sworn enemy.

One random shift of tracks can make you jolt back to reality, only for the longing to jump to get you.

Every lush field, every passing river, every dark tunnel, all signify a purpose. Every change of terrain, every change of wind on your face brings with it a multitude of thoughts. The 'what ifs', the 'hows' and 'whys', and probably the most nagging; 'how wills' and 'what wills'. You question the purpose of every traveller, and in the end, you agree, that each has his own destination, and they will try their best to reach it.

Nothing is assured, however. You never know when you might need to pull the chain, or jump out. Every time I cross a river while I am at the door, I want to jump. Too bad I can't swim. Not to say I would have jumped off if I could, but that remains on my bucket list.

To jump, to jolt, to chug, to halt, to move and to reach. That is a train journey and that, is life.

The Aesthetics Of Hypotheticals

Every ideal, every situation has its opposite. Pessimism is countered by optimism. Negativity is negated by positivity. Then there is this one ideal I've always been told as ideal; to be a realist. The *ideal* ideal. Realism, in the modern era, seems to be the cracking whip used by most – the elders, the accomplished, and the successful – to mould and shape a young mind the way the society and the world demands. They think that the child is too imaginative, naive and daft for it.

The idea of imagination is a curious one. It oscillates from being beautiful to self-damaging. As a child, you're expected to 'break open the shackles of conventional thinking' and 'use the endless possibilities of your mind'. Somewhere as you grow up; those demands decrease. You are expected to adjust into, settle into the definitions provided - rigid and uncompromising. The derivatives of one's imagination are used less and less, and the conscious leaves its efforts to create.

That's when the beauty begins. From where the conscious gives up, the subconscious picks up.

> *"In dreams, we enter a world that's entirely our own."*
>
> *– Albus Percival Wulfric Brian Dumbledore*

Some of the most nagging questions one faces are the 'what ifs' and 'how wills'. These often arise from scenarios built up in one's subconscious, which rarely match with the situations around you. You dream, you wish, you speculate, and you win. Somewhere, every young child's heroic wish is fulfilled. A very astute concept of it was laid out by J. K. Rowling in the *Harry Potter Series*, with the *Mirror of Erised*. The mirror would reflect your inner desires, what you want the most. Who doesn't want to be successful? To feel wanted? To be acknowledged, praised, loved and cared about? That's where imagination kicks in.

Imagination - it grips you, sucking you in like a black hole. A pleasurable black hole, because you control that simulation. You decide it's situations, you devise its events. You're either the hero of a perfect world, a champion of the underprivileged, you're with the one you couldn't be; or whatever your true feelings lay out for you. Dwelling in it, like spending hours in front of the *Mirror of Erised,* will take you away from the excruciating clutches of the reality for a while. You love to be there, you want to spend most of your time there. That's where the compulsive tendency becomes dangerous. As our friend did warn,

"It does not do to dwell on dreams,
and forget to live." – A. P. W. B.
Dumbledore

Excessive dwelling in the wishful world, a world of your own makes you obsessive about a world perfect for you. Such is the cruel tale of life. It is for everyone, yet nobody's monopoly. Its definitions change frequently, a little too quickly for an imaginative mind to adjust to it. When the differences between the hypothetical world and the real world become vast, that's when things start getting ugly. The shock of finding out that you may or may not be what you dream in reality, or what you have there vanishes here, after a long state of otherworldly trance can be difficult to adjust to. It can be as sudden as snatching away the crutches of a disabled person, leaving him unbalanced, unfocused and in pain.

The world of imagination is beautiful, but as most often said, too much of a good thing has to be bad. However, I'd like to call upon the wisdom of Albus Dumbledore one last time,

"Of course it's happening inside
your head, Harry, but why on earth
should that mean it is not real?"

**Quotes from the Harry Potter Series, by J.K. Rowling.*

Extending An Aiding Hand

No drowning man can know which drop of water will kill him. No one who ever lived and believed that he doesn't need help has been proven right. Help is something we all need. Help is something we all expect, yet often abstain from providing some.

Why do people refrain from helping others? When sometimes all you need to do is to be there, provide a listening ear, or lend a shoulder? The problem is we often mistake the term 'help' with the materialistic expectation of giving and taking things. It's the prospect of losing a prized item - however temporarily - that puts off any humanitarian and natural tendency of the person to lend help.

I've been often asked, "Why do you never say no to someone who needs help, even if they often run you over later?" My answer is simple. I say, "Have you ever been in a situation where you desperately need help, and there's no one to aid you? I've experienced that. The sheer helplessness, the uselessness and an apologetic numbness that grips you - I try not to heap that on someone if I can help it."

It is true; people do very often run you over after their need for support is exhausted. Over the years I have been run over and realised people have been run over too. Many seem to think that's how the vicious cycle of help goes. Yet when I look back at the people who have genuinely appreciated my help, I realise that contrary to what I've expected; I've come out richer than I was before. In most cases, I've made a good friend, a valuable acquaintance. Help should not be done to gain an upper hand on someone, or to reach a moral high ground. Help is not a countable thing, naming them as favours ruins the entire essence of your deeds.

The most effective of help is often to be a listening ear to a weeping friend at two in the morning. Or even to be a companion in the long, lonely wait someone has to do. Or to maybe just share a few words and make a person believe again in a dream, in an ambition. Because it's the possibility of having a dream come true that makes life exciting and worth living.

Help cannot, and should not be measured by numbers as in a profit and loss statement. Nor should it be done in a way that doesn't satisfy you or leave you questioning your decision.

Because help done which leaves afterthoughts is a weight on both the receiver and the doer.

An Ambiguous Balancing Act

The perfect alignment of your favourite wall piece. The right tinge of colour on an artist's palette. Just two spoonfuls of sugar - not more, not less - in your morning cup of tea. An equal amount of weight on both trays of the weigh scale. The right length of an essay - neither too lengthy, nor too short. Everything from the smallest of anecdotes to the largest of philosophies revolves around one ideology - balance.

Yang and Yin; Ma'at and Isfet; God and Satan. Spirituality has always, in one way or the other emphasized the importance of balance. To portray an everlasting battle between good and evil, it is essential to empower both equally. To craft one side good and the other evil, one needs a reference of negativity. In other words, God needs Satan just as much you need God.

Just like the classic 'Balancing on the Rope' act, everything hangs in a balance of sorts. Glories and defeats; happiness and sadness, popularity and loneliness - it all is necessary just in the right amount. Keenly observed, it comes out that everything is in our hands with nothing being in our control. The little girl walking on the tight rope is bombarded with unnerving, expectant and awed looks, the prospect of falling and the fear of a potential failure. These are the things beyond her control, yet she chooses to remain focused and puts forward strong foot after strong foot and finishes the act.

Balance is rarely easily achieved. It takes multiple tries, potential devastations and stretches of discomfort. Each one of us struggles to balance various events, factors and situations in our life; ranging from petty problems to huge feuds. When in distress, one often wonders about the apparent injustice, inconvenience or unfairness. It is our own tinted perception that wants everything aligned to our own selfish needs and greeds that actually magnifies any problem. We want to feel warm without knowing the bone creeping chill, we want success without tasting defeat, we want to love without the anguish of heartbreak. It is impossible to get the best of one without experiencing the other. True success is based on the foothills of failures, heartbreaks make you value not only the love you give, but more so the love you receive. There is a reason nature tries to balance the hours of day and night equally, but doesn't manage it every day. But when it does, we celebrate the equinoxes as a tribute to fairness. Quoting Rick Riordan,

"Fairness does not mean everyone gets the same, fairness means everyone gets what they need."

Understand yourself to be the centre of your own universe, with multiple ropes tied to your waist and extended in all directions. The end of each rope is attached to a sphere of life - friendship, love, hate, etc. The sphere tied exactly opposite is always the inverse counterpart. The sphere of happiness is opposite to the sphere of sadness. As each sphere demands attention, the sphere pulls the rope. As one pulls, the other feels the force as well. In the flow of life, multiple spheres will pull simultaneously, hence moving you away from the centre. No pull is permanent, and as the force ebbs away, the sphere opposite to it begins working to help bring you back to the centre. It may take time for all the pulls and all the forces to be in equilibrium and achieve utter control; maybe even a lifetime.

But you, at the centre, are not a puppet, nor a lifeless rock. You have your own powers, your own strengths. What can you do? You can fight to not be pulled by the negative forces, but also to not be carried away by the positive forces. You can hold firm at your base and refuse to budge, therefore leaving the balance to your hands. You cannot control the pulls of the spheres, but you can choose how to react to them and eventually reduce their impact. You control your placing. This state has been described differently like Nirvana, Moksha, Salvation etc. It's nothing but balance.

"Yeh Jo Gehre Sannate Hai, Waqt
Ne Sabko Hi Baanteni Hai,
Thoda Gham Hai Sabka Kissa, Thodi
*Dhoop Hai Sabka Hissa."**

MEANING: All the deep silences,
time has spread them to all;
Some sadness is everyone's tale,
some sunshine is everyone's share.

* *Javed Akhtar, Zindagi Na Milegi Dobara*

The Autopsy Of Assumptions

The day to day monotone of an individual often relies on unconventional methods to make it viable. Then again, conventionality is a relative term, with its definition changing as perceiver changes.

Considering the monotone as terrain, with peaks and valleys, plateaus and plains gives a handy idea. The valley following a peak may often be harmful. You can navigate that by either cutting off the peak; which unsurprisingly none of us want to; or by filling in the valleys. Perhaps the most common way to fill these valleys are the receiving of assurances, trust, love and appraisal. And none of the aforementioned gifts are guaranteed. So what does one do!? Either hit the floor hard or at least create a temporary cushion not exactly lasting, but good enough to absorb the fall? The cushion is often assumed.

I find the very concept of assumptions lazy. Everything about it is lazy. The process, the accusations, the benefits. I even refuse to accept it as a legitimate term. 'Assumptions', in my view is the greater roof which encloses the more astute subordinates - estimates, presumptions and conjectures. Granted, all three are based on incomplete information, but anyone with substantial experience of life knows that the probability of you knowing everything about something is next to zero. Somewhere, sometime, someplace; we all assume. You go to sleep every night assuming that your body will function properly all night so that you wake up well and alive. You assume that your family will love you, support you; that your friends will help you and that things will eventually be all right.

Every relationship to me is two people reading each other like a book. Reading the tales; the embarrassments, the triumphs, the happiness and the sadness. Of course, then come the shortcomings of how many chapters one opens up to someone. Someone may not want to be an open book, while some are. And when your counterpart is an open book, he needs your words to write a chapter about you in his story.

Consider it such, that your counterpart requires an emotional influx from you. It's a mandatory part of all deep, meaningful relationships. Now, he demands an influx at a rate quite faster than the rate you're willing to provide. That makes it difficult to be blunt and straight, and he does need answers. So in his mind, he has voids. He fills them with his next best option, judgment and assumptions - which are mostly based on close observation of your traits and behaviour. Since he has built temporary conclusions which many times he isn't consciously aware of, he refrains from poking for more influx. And as usual, you're inclined to keeping cards close to your chest. This creates a divide - something which happens to every relationship.

And the thing is if he assumes, he doesn't actually realise that he's doing it. For him, it's the absolute godly sense of self-righteous intellect that tells him that he's figured this out, and since from his viewpoint the gaps he has filled make sense, he declares them astute. As an aftermath, his notion about the relationship he shares with you becomes tinted, and he tries to fit everything into the narrative he has in his mind. And when one situation pops up which doesn't fit into the narrative, he ends up in a fix. Either he questions his narrative he is quite convinced of, or he confronts you.

You can end up astounded, amazed and often offended about the things he has assumed about you. In your own place, you have a right to be hurt and angry. But if you ask him to explain, as to why he made such assumptions, the things he may tell you can shake your world, and change how you look at yourself and often change how you portray yourself.

This doesn't happen in every relationship, of course. It takes a high level of understanding between the two parties to reach this level. Even assumptions need a platform of information, knowledge of the partner's smaller habits and obvious traits. Assumptions often create a domino effect, one small assumption paves way for bigger, larger assumptions to shoot in.

Such a situation is quite essential, to take your relationship to a deeper level. It's a mark of the strength of the bond between two people that one has the confidence to indulge and assume about the other, and believe that he/she is correct.

Assumptions are crude, and accusations of being assuming are rude. Let's not assume that the assumptions made are baseless, for you'd never assume that you may be at the fault as well. Assuming that – one is mature enough to talk out of a mess and make the initial assumption – that eventually everything is going to be all right - become a reality.

Giving It Time

If there is anything truly timeless, it is time. It is the initial starting point, the first God, an embossed quantity. It is a force stronger than any, a blanket encompassing everything; yet a subtle presence often unnoticed. Despite our efforts, we fail to quantify, measure and understand time. How can you hope to evaluate something you simply cannot outlive?

'Life is a race, if you don't run fast, someone will trample and overtake you.' This ever-popular line signifies how we view time. You need to clock the least time to win, but is it really that way? Is life a race where your success and happiness is a measure of how quickly you've achieved them? Over the years, man has learnt to use time as a tool to build a ladder to success. Make no mistake, time is the sharpest tool at your disposal. If used wisely, it can carve you a sensational piece of wonder whereas if used brashly, it can lead to detriment unique to it. However, as it is with any tool, keeping it untapped and unused will see it rust and spent. Spent or wasted time is as gone as the dead, a lesson most realise much late.

In the haste to go places, man has never enjoyed any place to its fullest. In the greed to get as much as he can, he's never truly appreciated what he possessed. In his ambition to move up, he never paid attention to what and whom he was crushing beneath. It is often contrived that you have very less time to make your career, or that opportunities come only a few times in a time cycle. Careers and success have become so synonymous with 'time management' that we fail to provide time where at times it is needed the most – often beyond our careers and workplaces. Many will say you don't have time. I say, take a breath. Give it time.

Give it time, because everybody needs it. Your time is not only yours, but it is also a bundle of the time and attention you've received which you need to give back. Busy is not something to be if busy means shutting down other people who need you now and whom you might need later. Humanity is our sinew, and it feeds on the time given. The demands are rarely high, just one message or an acknowledgement or an evening together can do wonders not only for the other person but for you as well.

Give it time, because no idea is truly golden. Ideas are many things; everlasting, revolutionary and yes, bulletproof to say some; but no idea is perfect. Your ingenuity may seem flawless, and it may seem easy to just start work on realising it without refining it. Yet, the more you search, the more improvements you can find, and more ways of avoiding future blockages. Ponder your ideas, shape them and then begin your actualisation. The more initial brain work, the less afterwards handwork. However, giving time does not mean pushing the deadlines further but starting early and doing your work proper justice. Everyone finds themselves at a crossroad, with the option of going back rendered invalid. Give time to choose your next path.

Give it time, because you are not flawless. Face the fact that you are fallible, and you can definitely make crucial mistakes. It is perceived that there is no time for mistakes, but there has always been time for mistakes. When held up, give yourself some time sort your errors out. Or maybe invest time in somebody else to sort it out. Brood over the solution, so as to make sure you never commit a similar mistake again, as a repeated mistake is the biggest waste of time.

Give it time, because you're not a saint either. Run-ins, differences of opinions and clashes are bound to happen. The right way to go about it is acquiescence, not accusation. The trajectory of accusation is a boomerang, some way or the other it is going to come back at you. Give yourself the time to think about your companion. Give time for the tribulations to wear down, for the rages to calm and for the initial displeasure to simmer down. But most importantly, give the others time. Exchange positions with your companion, place yourself in his/her shoes. Because if you know you have made a similar error before, you can prevent them from making one as well.

Give it time, because change is time oriented. We grow dissatisfied quickly, and demand change even more quickly. Change, by its very nature is not immediate. The more substantial the change, the more time it requires to come into effect. Unnecessary chipping and chopping is not going to help, let the decisions and efforts come into being. It's the 'fast food' culture that's hampering us. Slow down a little. Sometimes, it's good to see your efforts bear fruit. Enjoy your successes, because they have the power to change your future.

Give it time, because haste ruins more than patience stalls. Experience and wisdom come with giving things time. Experience is an assemblage of mistakes, and wisdom is the lesson the mind learns when the heart suffers. It all comes with time, and as they say, time heals everything.

Give it time, because your reserves are unknown, and regrets of the past have a nasty proclivity to suck the time from your present and eventually the future. Let's not fail to give time to a current need because we didn't manage to attend another one properly in the past. It is better to ponder today and sail tomorrow, rather than losing the shore and crying a wail of sorrow.

Give it time; because time can ripen the hues of life, paint them onto your personal canvas and create a masterpiece that deserves your worth.

Of Expectations and Satisfaction

'He walked on; the sack on his shoulders a mere trivial, avoidable distraction. The future in sight, the path beneath his feet, and a journey towards his goals to look forward to..'

The world around us has built up a compilation of needs and demands that it wishes to extract from an individual and has subtly named it expectations. So much so, that a person accepts, emulates and passes on the ideology without thinking about either the repercussions or pretext. Expectations vary from the realistic to the unrealistic; helpful to damaging; beneficial to borderline sadist. And the most common purpose of expecting? To be satisfied. In whatever manner - emotionally, financially, socially or materialistically.

'Walking on, on the horizon he could see his house. Home. Perhaps he could take a siesta there. He walked on. His parents and siblings were at the door, expecting him. He greeted them, asked them to let him rest a little. "No, son. You have duties to observe, education to do, job to get, and money to make. After all, you are my son, and you have to live up to me." his dad said. "Father's right," his mother echoed. "If you aren't stable, how can you support us in our old age? You must strive, you must prosper. That's the least we can expect, can't we dear?" The sack on his shoulders got substantially heavier.'

Everyone expects something from us, and in return, we expect something from everyone. It has become an unwritten rule, seldom challenged. The rule doesn't care about fairness, it just expects you to expect. Is it rarely a surprise that the people closest to you expect the most - whilst the relative strangers offer you more space? Many times it also happens to be the case that the nearest ones do not expect much, but that's seldom because of the right reasons. For it is often our own who underestimate us the most. The expectations in such situations do not really vanish, they just transform. They turn into expectations of hoping that you finally grow into someone they can expect other, greater, better things from. Yet, it's the love that exists that stops the imbalance from going haywire, and in the end, a family strives towards overall satisfaction - where everyone's expectations are fulfilled.

'He trudged on, trying to ignore the weight on his shoulders. Halfway through his journey, he had met a bunch of old friends he had inconvenienced by focusing on his career and his targets. They had accused him of being selfish and said what they had demanded was expected of a friend. He also came across the girl he loved, who expected to marry a different man in him. His shoulders were beginning to ache, and the weight was not ignorable anymore.'

The expectations of friends, whenever goes demanding and damaging is termed as peer pressure. Yet, peer pressure can be positive too. What do you do if your friends tell you not to give in to peer pressure? A troublesome scenario with circles and friendships - people come, people go. Memories remain. Even the scars, the bruises, and the wounds stay. The revolving door can get so painful to watch with the loneliness biting away. It would be like drowning in your own heart; slowly suffocating in your own blood, and the only way out would be to drill a hole and escape. Yet, on come a few who are meant to stay, who mean to stay and who do stay. They repair the holes, the wounds and bruises, and drain the bad blood from your heart. And then, the satisfaction follows.

'His pace had gotten slower, and the pain was massive. He couldn't keep a straight face, and looked around. Others seemed to be in discomfort too but made a better effort to hide it. Or maybe they weren't under so much weight after all..'

Everybody is expected to expect, and we come to expect ours and their expectations. Yet expectations of most are unique, their burdens specific. Often times I've looked at people on the street and thought I'd be jealous of at least one thing each of them has if I knew their tale. Then I realise that if I did know their tale, I'd be glad for a thousand things in my own life. That's how satisfaction seeps in. It's the weighing scale of expectations pending and expectations satisfactorily fulfilled that needs to be balanced. Naturally, some expectations are going to be left untouched and unfulfilled. And the ones fulfilled will soon be forgotten. That's the malice of this game, and everyone drinks of this chalice.

Satisfaction is not a matter of receiving, it is a function of giving. Fulfilling expectations gives more satisfaction than getting your expectations fulfilled. Yet it is never one way, and the balancing of incomplete expectations and satisfactorily fulfilled expectations' scale has to be two ways. The thumb rule or the motto should be, 'You fulfil one, I do the same. Together, we abandon some, and stay in a healthy relationship.'

'His body couldn't take it anymore. He collapsed at the place which was his destination, whether he liked it or not. This was definitely not the place he set out to reach. He never realised, that the weight he kept on adding on his shoulders gradually drifted him away. He could sense the reaper on his way, and thought; "They expected and expected.. and I strived to fulfil them," he mused; finally turning his withered face away, "but it is I, who dies truly unsatisfied."

The Acceptation of Exception

"Chemistry is a subject of exceptions;" my teacher began. She paced sideways towards the periodic table hung on the sidewall and continued, "Understanding the concepts behind these exceptions will help, not memorization."

As I doodled on my notebook page, I reflected on what she said. True enough, it's the exceptions that have always made the telling difference, rather than the monotone or the expected scheduling. How many times has the kindness of one man stood up against the cruelty of tens? Or the wits of one prospered over the foolishness of hundreds? Or how has the faith of one fared against the thousands who had given up?

My teacher went on about Xenon having some special properties which allowed it to form compounds even though it was a noble gas. Yes, of course, this analogy fits into reality as well. Exceptions are often the product of certain different abilities, unique to each which makes everyone an exception. Exceptions root from nothing less than stubbornness, patience and an iron-clad resolution of never giving up, among others. Funnily enough, the exact concept of exceptions is relative - what may be an exception to you may be a common phenomenon for the others. Yet it would be foolish to assume that one needs a special power, a special talent within oneself to stand out in a crowd. I have seen and believed that every human being has something different and unique in their skill set; it just needs proper introspection and belief to unleash that. But even more than that,

"It is our choices, Harry, that show what we truly are, far more than our abilities."

—J.K. Rowling, Harry Potter and the Chamber of Secrets

Your skills are just a tool to make you an exception. It is how you utilize them decides whether you're going to be an exception worth some positivity or negativity. Well planned conspiracy killed Julius Caesar, and the unnerving faith and oratory skills of Mark Antonio avenged him. Brutus' righteousness set him apart; but is he looked upon as reverently as Antonio? A tool cannot be good or evil - a knife is not evil in itself, it depends on the wielder.

Exceptions are not just decisions. They can be a circumstance, an event, or a trait. But probably the most troubling aspect of this is when you are affected by someone else's exceptional decision, circumstance, event or trait. It is vital to understand that they are as unique as yours, and as crucial and important to them as your calls are to you. Yet, we want our exceptional endeavours to be accepted while we don't open up to the possibility of accepting exceptions imposed on us.

In such a scenario, considering oneself as an eggshell proves to be a useful analogy. The shell is meant to be broken, you are meant to break; either from an inside peck or an outside whack. The outside whack feeds a hungry stomach while the inside peck gives a new life. In both the cases, the shell breaks, the insides pop out in different forms, and the results are both positive in their own amiable way. To someone who does not understand growth or development, this process would seem devastatingly gruesome.

Exceptions are encountered at every step. Every step can be an exception to someone or the other. They can be manufactured from anything; thoughts, aspirations, wishes…

"Finished with your daydreams, Vishvaraj?" my teacher's voice jolted me back to the reality. "Care to tell us what were you dreaming about?" she asked.

"Exceptions, ma'am. Just following up on what you explained."

She smiled, and I got the hint that she understood way more than what I expected to reveal.

The Transition

Between light and darkness; sandwiched between the sun and the moon; and trapped within day and night lie two phenomena which have engrossed gazers and thinkers alike - dawn and dusk.

We all know the day. It is the span of the twenty-four-hour clock when you can see what you're shown. It is when the world bustles into activity to hustle in the tussle of each's individual battles. It is when the normal people do their work, shuttling between the monotonous regimes of bounds they have twisted themselves into. It's run by the same sun that fed your ancestor and feeds you too. The day; is the white.

Let me tell you about the night, the night I know. It is the span of the twenty-four-hour clock when you actually try to see things with your eyes. When the world settles into the confines of their comfy beds, aberrant people like me try to think their way out of the bounds we find ourselves in. It's signified by the same moon which was gaped at by many a poet and lovers over generations, myself included. Since you know not much about it, let's call it the black.

But they aren't exactly the two sides of a coin. Day and night don't flip into each other, they transform. And the transformations are called daybreak and twilight. They are the zones when both lose their rigid properties and just for a while, mix into each other. If you're normal, you often miss it. You miss the first wave of warmth after a cold night or the first cool breeze after a hot day; with the sky bearing a fantastic palette of scarlet, crimson, orange, yellow and blue; full of activities of the winged marvels. You miss the satisfaction of knowing how and when your day passed or why you are awake as the day breaks.

It's those blurry areas between extremes, the actual spectrum between the ends of a spectrum, the swish of the pendulum. Transitions have always played an important role in every aspect of life - changing, building, growing - developing things, people, relationships and emotions.

Did I say emotions? Sure then, let's see the spectrum of emotions.

The ends of the spectrum are pretty well documented.

The sheer force with which the tide of emotions flow in; sweeping every deed, chore and productivity in its path. The volume of it is so massive it renders time useless, reduced to the mere ticking of the clock. The pull, which is futile to resist, easily takes you to places you left but didn't really move out from and even more easily reopens scars mildly tapered upon. Scars, which burn the more you drown in the swamp, like salt on raw live flesh. You feel you're holding up the sky, with your hair greying quicker than ever. You question everything you've done, every stance you've stood for, every decision taken and every reaction given. Nobody has time for you, loneliness vests deep into your soul. You feel there's no bigger monster in this world than you, that everything is your fault, and that the world is a better place without you.

And then there are some days wherein you release yourself from every pillar ever tied to you. That absolute feeling of carefree carelessness when a respectful shamelessness seeps into your being. Your happiness seems ineffable, unbreakable and it just radiates off you wherever you go. You feel on top of the world, liberated from everything that ever held you back, free as a winged marvel. You just don't care about the wrongs in the world, you don't care if you've erred somebody, you don't feel lonely because you have your time and attention for yourself. You feel there's love, in you around you, but most vitally important, for you. The world beams of colours you've never seen before sings tunes you've never heard before and laughs with you to things meant to tickle you forever.

But you know what both the ends are. How they both feel.

Ever felt that you have neither, but need either of the two ends? Or that you're in such a grey that you need neither the white or the black? Ever noticed that both - exhilarating happiness and excruciating pain have their own weird pulls? Ever wondered how sadness can have a pull? Ever realised, that you actually have a choice here to make? You either choose the daybreak or the twilight. Since you're normal, you'll choose the daybreak.

You choose happiness. You choose it in spite of the fact that it requires a certain level of wilful ignorance. You ignore the wrongs done and the bad happenings because you know of ten more rights done and good things done. You let things go because your soul can't bear to be weighed down. So you approach happiness. From your monotone you cannot break out of, you seek small pleasures. You treat every small pleasure as a treasure, and you are more than willing to share your treasures. You try to make sure you have a genuine smile on your face, and you make sure to pass it on. You choose it, so you drag yourself from the shackles of the grey nothingness and scamper towards your happiness. And that is when you realise that happiness isn't the smile on your face, it is the smile you give to someone else's face. You understand that happiness isn't your treasure, its sharing the said treasure. You grasp that happiness isn't the end of the spectrum, it is the work towards it. Happiness isn't the white, it is the part just before it. Happiness is the transition. Happiness is daybreak.

Me, however, I don't choose happiness at times.

I often have a compelling love for the lure of sadness. The alcoholic love of pain, of desolateness, of the sad melancholy filling your ears. My soul prefers to stay down and look at things in their crudeness, rudeness and crassness. I don't try to pull away from the grey, instead, I let it slide me into shades growing darker and darker. I see things the way they are – rugged, rocky and raw. And however as much I feel like addressing them, I know it's not going to change. The cotton can't cut the rock, no matter how thick. And the rock can't be sewn into cloth, no matter how slender it is. So I let the black pull me in. But it is the black for a reason, and it doesn't take me in completely. I can only get closer and closer, but never really reach it. It's almost like the black is a place I feel I belong, yet at times it leaves me with a pit in my stomach which yells of not belonging anywhere. Nevertheless, I look forward to darkness, yet I struggle to find it. I am trapped in twilight.

Because we don't know what actually 'the white' is, but 'the black', is definitely death.

A Tribute To Solitude

It was raining outside; heavily, but not harshly. The dark clouds had made the afternoon sun vanish and the daylight had dimmed as if nature had a sudden case of low voltage. I sat there, with a book in my lap, gazing out of the window at the sour sky and watching the raindrops lash against the window rim. Once a while an audacious droplet would charge to attack my face and even more rarely, one infinitesimal drop would make it. I closed the window, pulled the curtains; dipping my room into a familiar shade of darkness - perfect for brooding, reflecting and concocting.

I settled myself on my bed, leaned back and waited. Waited for the tide to flow in, and retreat leaving behind memories I thought I had dumped forever. Before I could decide what to do with those awash memories, new waves would flow in, bringing a new charge with them. I had been here before, and I shall be here again. I decide to walk on the shore of thought and choose memories that will tear into me today. I had given in to the cascades of solitude.

Solitude - an imaginary mind's paradise, a rational mind's school. It is an exception, yet a humdrum of everybody. Solitude isn't loneliness, it's not the despair of lack of companionship. Solitude is embracing the loneliness, finding peace in the quiet, settling your self with respect to yourself, and setting yourself free. Loneliness turns into seclusion, which yields solitude. In solitude, I found myself. It gave me a scope to unleash both, the angels and demons within me. Unrestrained, uncontrolled, and unbounded, I let them shape me. Soon I was in a quandary - should I negate my demons or pamper my angels?

I remembered my first foray into the spiral of solitude. Realisations and it's crude holdings had freshly struck me, putting myself in a null. It was the first time I let my thoughts run amok, and run wild they did. I took it all in, from the lack of invites to the cordial ignorances - the first blow of loneliness is always the strongest. Somewhere between a forearm covered in ribbons and bands on Friendship Day during school and sitting alone, listening to music and reminiscing about the past, I grew up. My memory had nothing but bitter rejections, cut-offs and a feeling of hostility - all completely unwarranted.

It's quite funny actually, how ninety-nine people would give me compliments and one person would say something negative; and I would end up spending hours on that one negative comment without even giving a second thought to the ninety-nine praises. In my initial forays into solitude, I had no control over my cognition - I let myself believe that I was always disgraced, left alone and unattended. I made trust my mythological Holy Grail - while it was nothing but a smile away from me.

Sometimes it's trust that makes you trustworthy. When someone trusts you, you feel to start trusting yourself. I remembered how I found it difficult to trust someone until somebody else trusted me. Somebody else's trust which I couldn't honour. And at that moment, all the times when my trust was broken seemed irrelevant. It didn't matter how many times I was wronged, I had eventually done the same wrong to someone else. How could I blame someone else for doing to me the same crime I did to many others? I was no different than my culprit, and I had now become a criminal myself. How badly I wanted to turn the clock back in actuality, not for revenge, but to correct an error made in an innocuous moment.

Oh, life! What a sneaky little pest it is! The perpetrator of an event I try my best not to hold a grudge on to, it shows to me every single day. The face I wanted to express to and couldn't, never crosses my path again.

I gained control – learned to control my demons a little, and gave true flight to my angels. I acquired their solace, I listened to their teachings. I realised, that I had started wrong, but on the most common path. I realised that I had a choice between misplaced negativity and possibly reaching a higher level of sense and maturity. I understood that you can allow your pain to do two things; either let it fool you or let it fuel you. I decided to no longer answer the complaints of my heart, instead, I started asking it counter questions.

We have always asked the wrong questions. We ask, what makes someone love? Or what causes happiness? Or what causes a sense of success? Actually, all these are default, initial or perceived situations of human life, they're not caused – particularly the latter one. A baby, a toddler is loved by almost everybody who sees it and is happy and excited about the smallest victories of life. From the first chortle to the first word; and the first step. The real questions, then, are what causes hate? Or what causes sadness or what causes disappointment? Why is it, that we're all apart, tearing more and more into our own – at the bare minimum – biological kin? It's a shame that humankind has progressed along the lines of 'survival of the fittest or smartest', like other animals. With our ability to think better, our crimes became more heinous. Had we progressed along the lines of 'survival of the ethical', or even 'the righteous', we'd be living in a totally different world right now, which may not be perfect, but vastly different.

Nowadays, I seek salvation in solitude. Gone are the days when I would accuse, whine, feel sorry for myself and play the victim. I now think about ordinary things in life.

An incident with my father taught me a lot. When I was a kid, we used to travel in our car with me often in the front seat. Once, I saw a huge pothole in front of us and braced myself for the inevitable crash into it. I closed my eyes and waited and waited, but the drop never came. I opened my eyes and saw that we had passed the crater without any problems.

"Dad, what happened to that huge pothole?"

"We passed it, son."

"But how didn't we fall in it? It was big, and just in front of the car! "

Dad smiled, "We did go over it. The thing is, the car did; the tyres didn't."

Years later, I realised something. We are a vehicle on the road of life. Our tyres are our pillars, things and/or people closest to us. Whatever craters and bumps we encounter on the road, they represent the problems and frenzies of life. You must negotiate the bumps with your tyres in full harmony or even the positives can become uncomfortable. More so, you must protect your tyres while encountering the craters. Sometimes, dipping into a crater is inevitable, and it must be handled with care, approaching it with caution. Your car runs on your tyres, you need to protect them. Similarly, take care and handle your pillars with care because help you stay up and make progress during both, positives and negatives. But sometimes, you need not worry, as you'll pass over the pit without your pillars even knowing it.

The rain had not subsided, and neither had my thoughts. I knew it could go on and on and on, but I was now the commander of my solitude. My Solitude Angel agreed, and I closed the session, succumbing to sleep. But once in a while, I do let my demons get some fresh air too; just to keep it interesting.

A TRYST WITH TRUST

"

A string of letters, a yarn of words;
Truths and lies and sayings of sorts.
Knitting together a tapestry of swords;
Feeling and fueling the flames of hordes."

Honours were at stake, a war was to be fought. A murder was to be avenged, justice was to be served. When Mark Antony began his speech at Julius Caesar's funeral, it was more than a friend giving a eulogy to a fallen friend, or a disciple seeking justice over an assassination. Shakespeare's pen had created the ideal stage to understand how the conundrum of trust worked, ranging from the exclamatory realisations of rupture ("*Et Tu, Brute?*") to its salvation. But it made one thing quite clear to me - that trust feeds on words. Or maybe words hold an invisible control over trust. I haven't quite decided yet.

How does one explain trust? Is it the seamless transition from frivolous titter tatter to deep exchanges of one's inner hues? Or maybe it is the safety bracket of a certain presence, always there? I don't actually agree completely with any of these. Trust, for me, is the sincerity in a promise, the knowledge of one's needs, the value in a relationship and the fear - yes, fear - of abandonment or drifting away. In other words, when we are at the sea of life, trust is the oar which drives you to a shore.

"The sea was selfish, he could have sworn;
Doesn't let you swim with the crown.
But as shortly as you're dead and forlorn;
Nor even will it let you drown."

How ever changing is the definition of trust for some. Some days, it is the fulfilling of needs; while on the other it is the righteousness of deeds. Why does our idea of trust throw us into a cocoon of hiding? Yes, trust is meant to be a strength, a protective armour to watch one's back. But it isn't meant to hide us from the ones we want to trust and ourselves! The act of 'breaking of trust' is more used as an accusatory threat or a manipulative jibe these days. Trust is a double-edged sword which can be very helpful as well as very harmful. Trust is an animal which can be the most ferocious in war - by the virtue of its stability and also because of its potential of damage due to betrayal - but once tamed into your dealings, it will catch you when you're falling and push you up when you're drowning.

Trust is something which can only be truly shared in its full potential when you trust yourself. So when you enter a relationship and talk about trusting someone, never mistake it with the other person being a dump yard of your feelings and experiences you don't want to deal with. 'How, and whom to truly trust?', I found myself asking. And the answer came to me in a swift swirl of mundane inspiration - the heart, the mind, the eyes. School only managed to teach me that the eyes are for reading things, the mind is for learning and the heart is for pumping. Life taught me that the eyes can be read, the mind can be learned from and that the heart can bleed too. Trust these three, and they will teach you to trust.

"Loaded with loads and loads of loads;
With the weight threatening to disembody.
For the dead man in the dead sea showed;
The weight was life, not the body."

Life has it's fulcrum gently positioned around the people in your life. People adapt, accept, tolerate, appreciate and worship people. There will be many people who will adapt for you. That, however, doesn't mean they accept you. Also, if someone says they tried to accept you but refrain from telling you whereupon you can improve, they haven't really accepted you. Acceptance does not mean mere tolerance, and it surely does not mean that change cannot be induced with acceptance. Figuring out where you stand in the lives of others gives you a fair idea of your own placing.

There are always going to be only a handful of true friends - no matter how many people you know and how huge your coteries are. Someday when the call comes, and you do realise that people are not what they told you they were, or not even what they decided to show you they are, sit down and reflect. Reflect not on what you could have done better with them, but on how you can do better than them. Let the tears flow, if they come. Tears and time are the brothers of a new start, a clean slate. Tears are nature's time-turners. When it comes to people, the sands of time shall wipe things away and after you clean the sands, you have a clean slate, ready to be drawn upon again. Time doesn't however, balm the cracks on you. It only dries them out, so they're rendered lifeless, sometimes to be cut open again.

"If faith can move mountains, say oh lord!
Why tempt, build and mould evil?
Afraid about who will pray to you, god;
If there was no devil?"

I have often thought about an audience with someone who knows what I don't as a chat till eternity. And safe to say, I've found bits and pieces of such chats in humans, nature and myself. So according to that notion, an all-knowing God is nothing but all knowledge divided finely into each living being. That is because if you have the knowledge, you take actions. You take actions, you make errors, you get wisdom. Nothing earns you more wisdom than the shenanigans of the Game of Trust. Wisdom is a reservoir of knowledge which knows when to come up to the surface. True wisdom catches most people unawares, mostly the protagonist. Thus, for me, this is the idea of an all-knowing entity, because if an action taking God did exist, I doubt he would be rather happy with the current world's affairs.

"The lone nomad of the fading night;
Prepares to say adieu in the morning.
For what he tried to say with all his might;
Was all to be mistaken as mourning."

Actions and deeds do define the shades of trust, but if there is one ideal which has a very interesting connection with trust, it's honesty. Deep down I feel that we're living in a Stone Age, repeating itself. It's just that I prefer a Stone Age where our tools were stone and hearts were flesh, rather than our hearts stoned and tools being flesh. Honesty and trust have a very queer relationship - trust inspires honesty and honesty gives back substance to trust. Honesty is the best policy. It may not be a mass appealing and appeasing one, but it sure leaves you with no conscience driven what ifs. However, it also isn't a regret proof policy. It sure does give you a fair share of regrets. But the power of honesty to be sturdy in a storm and fluid in disturbances is crucial in a trusting relationship.

Trust is one of man's foremost requirements in love and happiness. These three are intertwined like the sky, stars and the earth, even the earth looks up to find the stars, and the sky has its need to protect the earth. Trust finds it's way into love and life, just the way words find a way into a writer's soul. A writer hides in his words like a caterpillar in its cocoon, like a joey in its mother's pouch, like a lover in his beloved. Life's games are hot and fiery, but none like the one man plays since he is born, the day he makes a tryst with trust.

"***Falling and stumbling, he is done;***
Charred and burnt and ripe with thirst.
'Cause life plays a fiery game with some;
For they've made a tryst with trust."

All Strings Attached

She is the face of experience; patron of existence; an embodiment of destiny. Gliding and touching every life on its way, playing hide and seek with everyone who seeks it out, she lays out her lessons with paramount ease and her teachings with adherent subtlety. 'Life', as many call her, has set an eye on the curious case of another girl, a mirror image of herself...

The baby gurgled and wailed; finished with sleep and on to hunger, two of the initial and foremost attachments 'Life' has deemed necessary for one and all. The little one has a lot of life in her and has a long journey to trod.

Infancy. The beginning of so many things, the decided staring point of a vicious cycle of events, joy, sadness and even more. A small child only cares about it's three primary needs - food, sleep and health - three attachments never to be let go. I look back at myself as an infant and get a pang of jealousy - such innocence, such awe at the smallest things yet an astute determination to do whatever I could to get what I want..

The child, learning and walking, reaching out to its parents for support and guidance. Ah, parenthood – the most beautifully disquiet experience 'Life' has managed to procure. Certain strings are meant to be attached and meant to stay that way.

Never has been a more beautiful relationship than a mother and daughter. I can remember so many times I looked up to my mother, for almost everything - guidance, counselling, beauty tips, behavioural and social sense, food, support, care and love. To be a mother is like one's is every daughter's aim, and irrespective of whether it transcends to a progressive chain or not, the feelings and admiration are always passed down from generation to generation. Mothers and daughters are like the Sun and the Earth – one all giving, the other glad to receive and utilize. And of course, the Earth acts as a mother to millions of us, maybe hoping that it can give as much as it receives from the Sun.

If the mother-daughter relationship is surreal, the father-daughter relationship is often surreptitiously deep and uniquely affectionate. The father is the daughter's first protective hand, her first hero, her first love. But for the father – the little darling is the most precious thing he has ever known, a pure angel with the power to heal with touch and smiles. Fathers and daughters are like the Earth and the Moon, daughter's life revolves around the father every day, and every movement in the daughter's life creates tides in the father's heart.

School, study, friends, colleagues, bullies - the little girl is meeting new and new people every day. The quandary of whom to trust and whom to not; and whether to tie the strings of attachment to one and all or to none but one? She must learn to decide, judge, protect her little heart, but it can sometimes only be learnt from experiences.

Friendship encompasses every emotion one can hope to encounter, either one at a time or all at once. Love, share, care, envy, jealousy, support, pressure, competitiveness – the entire package. It takes perseverance and a measure of highs and lows, knockdowns and lift ups and the shrinking of a void to really know the variants of your true friends. There were people who were always my merry chitter-chatter friends, while some considered me their SOS, but there were a couple of them, who took me in for what I was and accepted, tolerated and loved me for what little I had to give, and for the selfish tonnes I wanted to take.

But there were many I tried to build things with, to create a fortress often fabled in stories popular. I dug in, compromised and stayed when probably I should have let go. It was only when the string I held on to tightly began to sting that I realized that letting go was the better option - however much the decision hurt. Inherently, Lady Life taught me that only the effortless bondings travel long, or maybe we need to put ourselves first at times. People come, people go. If you don't lose, you don't grow.

She's a woman now and has fallen for someone she possibly cannot overcome. The shenanigans of Cupid strike again, and possibly one heartbreak among many can build the strength to differentiate herself.

Funny isn't it? How you keep one stand of attachment protected for that special one and when he finally arrives, you realize that your strand is made of satin and his' is nylon - never to be tied tightly. And then you question whether satin can only be tied to satin, or maybe the simple cotton - often overlooked do the trick?

Love breaks. It shatters. It makes you look at yourself in a way you've never seen yourself before. It builds in you a strength that takes quite some breaking, but it also unleashes a power hitherto uninitiated. But more so, it teaches you the difference between the two - strength respects, power intimidates.

Yet I did find solace and love, just not from the source I thought I would. The strings of mine once snipped which I rendered too short now were met with some with longer lengths of his. Love will find a way. Always.

Oh, Lady Life. You took away people and things I once couldn't live without; you cut the strings with someone I believed was the one for me. What have you tied me to, I ask?

The mature me looks back and sees myself tied to my parents, the basic needs, some true friends and a person I believe you presented to me for being a good girl all my life. Beyond that, I tied myself to my career, success and my children - just extending the knots of my parents. I am utterly thankful, for you knew which strings to cut and which to keep, even if I didn't agree with you in the immediate aftermath. But couldn't you have done it without this much pain which you decided to give?

The woman is now wise and has the teachings along with the lessons of life. Yet the child within her cannot see that teachings gave you intelligence, and lessons gave her wisdom. Oh, dear child of mine,

I am life, and I was teaching you how to live.

Highly Haughty Honesty

The old man sat in his rocking chair, his spectacles on his forehead and his hands clasped on his chest. He seemed lost in the paracosm of his thoughts when he was interrupted by his son, who looked visibly troubled. The old man straightened and asked what the matter was. His son shared the problems he had with his better half, and asked for advice. The father replied, "The answer is honesty. Its variations may differ, so may it's intensity, but the answer is always honesty."

"Can you explain?"

"Sure can. Let me tell you a story of me, your' mother, and of course, honesty."

We were together, yet distinct. Free in essence, yet intertwined with each other. We were like the sketch of a painting with the colours yet to be filled in, everybody could see that we were going to be grand. But sometimes, the colours that fill in aren't exactly the ones you want to see.

There comes a blip and tough times in every relationship. When one feels they need more than he is getting, things go wrong. In my need of filling that void, in my bid for her to accept my selfish needs, I launched what I thought was honesty at her. Honesty isn't about giving everybody a piece of your mind. Nor is it dishing out what you think of others. Honesty in its true sense is being true to yourself, acknowledging what you think of yourself and putting out words that you think that will help the other person as best as possible - keeping in mind your own conscience. My selfish needs made the relationship toxic, and things went downhill.

Somehow the times changed. We began to drift apart. The sad thing about two people drifting apart is that it can only happen when they are close. She went from being the safety locker of my deepest emotions to being a random open suitcase with all my secrets. She was a flower, and I was in love with her fragrance. Learn to keep the colours of the flowers in mind, son, because their fragrance is nomadic - it'll get lost on your journeys. When I once thought she was going to be the force behind my rise, instead I made myself believe that she was the reason I was in a storm. In a way, she was. I ran about, in the storm of my own chaos. I scraped and dug, plummeted and resurfaced, tried to hold my ground to reach the centre of the storm; only to see her wreaking havoc. Yet, from the centre, the storm sounded music, and she was the choirmaster. Little did I know that all I had to do was get into the heart of the problem, and things would be normal.

It took time. Honesty was moulded into a queer shape in me, defined to suit my own whims. I took it as a weapon to attack with and rarely as a shield to defend myself - that's the thing with people who are honest with everyone. They struggle to be truly honest with themselves. And when you aren't honest with yourself, your outward honesty is powerless. It can only bring discomfort. I asked her for help. I wanted to get rid of my worries and pain. I let them into a kite and asked her to release it into the wind, but in the end, they always remained connected to me by a single, sharp, cutting thread. She had become apprehensive - maybe we can't go back to what we had because we are no more what we were.

I accused her to be too innocent and naive, while it was me who was immature. The difference between innocence and immaturity is a sense of entitlement, an idea of self-righteousness and a notion of subtle vanity. My immaturity brought me unwarranted sorrow, you know, and I asked myself, "Did I really know her - or myself - in that matter?" Knowing someone is an illusion. There will always be that one streak of someone which remains concealed, something they themselves cannot be honest about. For long I maintained about honesty being a precursor of wisdom. I took intelligence for wisdom. Maybe you go about being intelligent but don't know about it? Knowing about one's intelligence is superficial. True wisdom catches most people unawares, mostly the protagonist, and so does honesty.

Often times I wanted to curl into a ball, to turn my heart into stone and render my emotions remorseless. I tried to protect my heart by pretending that I was heartless. And there was no bigger fallacy than that. But however much I tried, she ended up melting my heart, making me repent and setting me straight. She taught me a lesson in being myself. I finally became honest to myself and sought her out, to talk and to smoothen the creases. We sat down again, and as the cold, frozen conversation revived; all feelings, affection and memories came rushing back. Her style, her laugh, her smirk and her movements brought back the tides of everlasting love. They reminded me that my honesty wasn't really honesty, but it was a bunch of lies I told myself and to her to make myself feel better.

She made me love being in love. She made me fall through the stars and across galaxies, soar into the oasis of love and taught me the silent language of love. She showed me that the heartless gravity could pull you into the hearts of many. She made me write. I wrote poetry for her. But little did I know that she lived the poems I could not write and I wrote the poems she would not live. She was someone who touched even a cactus with love; many heartless people crush flowers beneath their feet. In my penance, I showed her my true face of honesty. I crumbled down my barrier of highly haughty honesty, and began to develop myself into something better.

She forgave me, with the grace only love can grant, and with the ease, only attachment can allow. And there we were, finally as a painting completed, with different colours than we intended to fill, but exquisitely grand nonetheless. We were together with ourselves, and we celebrated with a largely awaited kiss. The heartbeats fastened as the kiss slowed, the breaths coincided and we were there, in the paradigm of honest love.

His son looked searchingly. Somewhere within himself, he scrounged for that one piece of truth he had been hiding, which would make him a better person to tackle his situation.

'Dad,' he asked. 'What if I have already done my best? What if I can't improve?'

The old man smiled, 'You're ever changing, ever developing, and forever improving; son. You can never have a definite answer to the question, "What are you?"

*You only have a definite answer to the question when you're **dead**.'*

Roads Diverged In The Wood

"

Many roads diverged in the yellow wood,
Shall he take the weathered one, as the mellow would?
Or burst behind the mob, as the callow would?
Cautious and dwelling, the fellow stood."

I stand at a crossroad. No, it's a junction. It is a spray of paths that lie before me, splitting into a hundred directions in front of me; each pulling me tenaciously. From my feet springs a new path, a new possibility at every second thought. I hold on, barely, like a charioteer trying to keep a chariot drawn by a hundred horses in shape and direction. But I cannot linger, I cannot halt. The past is an abyss, a black hole sucking through, getting stronger at every passing second. All I have is this moment, the present. And I have to choose.

Somebody wise once told me that, 'everyone shall definitely face three things in life, a soul tearing choice, a heart-wrenching test and a distinct rock bottom failure; in that particular order.' The past is simple; the present, complex; and the future, indecipherable. There are some distances - the most crucial of them all - which must be travelled alone. That is a trod of vigour, bravery, hope, faith and endurance, but before that, you have to choose the path, and even before that, you prepare yourself.

How I ended up in the woods was never the question. I knew that I was not one of the box, even though I made a thousand efforts to blend in. I knew that I had both; my destiny and destination outside of the conventionality of my immediate society. It was opportune, that to reach a point where I was truly allowed to dictate my choices and would be held responsible for my decisions; I would have to walk the conventional path. I was destined for the woods, it was just that I took the cab to reach there. However, what matters is the journey I undertook to reach that point where I had a say, to and for, myself.

It is all a gameplay of destiny and destination. You may be destined to reach a destination, or the destination is not a part of your destiny. Often, life makes you choose - destiny or destination. Janus, the two-faced god alters your paths in a way that allows you to take control and move away from your destiny, a paradox which when you think about it, has plenty of examples to support it. Few manage to outwit Janus into choosing both - the destiny and the destination. My destiny was to conform to conventionality, my destination was to sprout my creativity, build it, create another scenario for Janus to try me, and beat him again. At least, that's the plan.

The woods. My journey till the woods was an ode to love and disregard, friendship and loneliness, gratitude and intolerance, hues and greys, fullness and emptiness, and guts and glory. I realised the lessons I needed vastly, both the easy and the bitter ways. I affirmed principles and morals that will act as my armour and my weapons, and most crucially, I realised that it is all a matter of cycles - up and down, troughs and crests, highs and lows. Things and deeds come around, actions and intentions are as different as hail and thunder. I have lived far too long in the darkness to not appreciate the light.

So here I stand. At the end of my conventionality, into the light woods, with a multitude of pathways in front of me. I know where I want to go. I don't know which way is it though.

I know where is my end point, I don't know which direction it lies in. I know my haven, but I know not which path will lead me there. I know I want to go to my goal, but I don't know if I will be able to make it.

How does it work? Does the end justify the means? Or the means validate the adherent failure to get to the end? What do I focus on, the road or the target?

The heart beats, the mind whispers. Reason says left, conscience says right. Janus stands here, once again. Funnily enough, I look back to my destiny for my answer.

Conventionality. society and its norms may not all be for me, but I have learnt a lot from what I did expose myself to. It taught me that it is sometimes just a matter of taking a step, the first step which marks the beginning of something great. Take things slowly. If you know your destination, and your next step, you should be fine. Sometimes it will be a cascade of choices, many times you will fail and will need to give it time. Break things down, listen to your heart. Play the game of trust. Seek out, and lend a helping hand. Be honest to yourself, your principles and your goals. Seek out love. Immerse yourself completely in the ones you love. Stay in love. Balance reality and imagination. It is a journey. Never mince your words. And in the end, irrespective of other's definitions of beauty, your life will truly be beautiful!

Conventionality taught me how to be unconventional. In a world where everyone wants to be different, it is crucial to be original. What I thought were blockages, became my stepping stones. The path next needs to be which caters to my love and my aim – irrespective of any other diversions. I laud those factors which pushed me towards the 'boring' conventionality, they taught me the difference between uncommon and unique.

They taught me that I was uniquely similar to billions, but similarly, uniquely, only one of myself.

I smile. I know my way.

What do we say to the god of gates, doors and pathways? 'I choose my way.'

"Many roads diverge into the woods, and I know which one I want to travel on!"

TÊTE-À-TÊTE

The cool breeze hit my face and ruffled my hair, as I bent on my balcony railing sipping my midnight tea. The serene city lights, mingled with some motion and sparse commotion were a sight to behold. The city never sleeps, and never truly, do we.

I was lost in my thoughts and queries, and I didn't notice that she was beside me.

'Hey,' she said softly.

I turned, and smiled, 'Hey.'

'What are you occupied with?'

'Myself, and my troubles..'

'Would you like to talk about them?'

Why not? Maybe talking about them will help. The questions and disconcerting negativity that were always around me, and maybe talking about them could solve some of their mystery. The negativity trapped me around like a spider's prey wound up in it's strong and sticky silk. The more I tried to squiggle out of it, the tighter it grasped. As each day passed it seemed to engulf me more and more, and I feared one day I would suffocate through it. But, how do I begin explaining myself?

She seemed to read my mind. 'I'll start, shall I?' She asked. I nodded.

'I think it all rests in the way we live our lives,' she said. 'Maybe we have just broken down life as a chore, while it has to be lived as a whole.'

'As in, broken down our responsibilities and duties? Divided our life span into ages?'

'That, and maybe more. We break down everything, we think it will give us answers. Science certainly has it that way. We think the smallest piece of our duties, responsibilities, spheres, habits may be the most crucial; ignoring that we and our lives are much much more than the mere sum of their parts.'

'You mean, the more modern we become the more we fail to understand life?'

'To an extent. Our life's motives have deviated from making the most of what results and outcomes we get, to striving for a predefined outcome. And therein, somewhere within that transition, we lost our understanding of life.'

'I don't know.. I always wanted a happy, peaceful and loving life. I've tried to make the best of what I've got, even though I may not be very happy about it. I just want the best... How have I deviated then?'

'Ah. You know what, things we desire the most often arrive a little dull and bland when they do. Why? Because in our desires and dreams we keep no true logical boundaries. We tend to put aside absolute reason and work towards fantasies. We design and craft such an impossible product that we never realize that we are often designing our own magnitude of disappointment.'

I took that in. Was I a little less realistic and a little overenthusiastic? Maybe. At times. But I had the details, I knew what I wanted and heck, I even knew how to get it. And if I did have lofty desires of my rewards, what's wrong? But yeah, my expectations do make me want more and enjoy what I have less. Maybe I tried to lap a hollow inspiration around with fancy words, and it just crumpled. The disappointment.. it gave a dose of negativity like none other.

'But, even if I fail or things don't turn out as I wanted them to, is it wrong to feel disappointed then?'

'Of course not. Feeling disappointment is fine, as long as you use it to grow and fight.'

'When I failed, and I had to face those who had invested in me, I took in their snides and their retorts. All I could see was negative things all about me. People never said a good word about me.'

'A lotus isn't polluted by the muddy waters. A submarine isn't affected by the salt water around it. A spaceship doesn't let the emptiness around it bother it's functioning. It doesn't matter what's around you. The problem starts when either the salt water enters the ship or the air inside the spacecraft leaks out. Do not let the outside negativity sink you and never allow your inside positivity to drain out to emptiness.'

'But you know,' I said, frustrated. 'I just don't seem to pin the problem. I feel forbidden to some things. I feel there are ways to do things, methods to deal with things with... I seem to never be, you know, free. I feel I'm always in a constraint. I don't like many things, and when I do I feel uneasy to share them! And it's like I am supposed to be so and so and I cannot be anything else! You getting me?' I looked at her, hoping she would grasp my question truly in my desperation.

She smiled, 'You know what the problem is? The problem is that we define a lot. We define what kind of humour we like. We define what kind of music we enjoy. We define what kind of love we want. We define what life we want to live. We strictly define what we like and what we don't like, and when something breaks that definition, it short circuits our functioning. Stop categorizing your pleasure and wants. If you like something, you like it. If you don't like something, you don't like it. You are not obliged to like something just because you've liked something similar in the past. You are not supposed to dislike something just because you've disliked something similar in the past. Maybe then you're in a different state of mind, in a different setting. You can like black as well as white. You have no obligation to be something, except to be the best of you. Things are simple. Let them be.'

Again. The same gist. Take it in. Keep it simple.

'Yeah. You know, what I don't get is, why is there some or the other fight always on? Why is there no real happiness? Or peace, for that matter?'

'I think that's because, for every true cause, there are multiple agendas. Do you know what trips me every time? That we chose to live by agendas, not ideals. We drag everything – small or large, frivolous or crucial, obvious or hypothesized – to fit our agendas and their predispositions. We create stories out of thin air, we stretch facts so much into thin layers that it hardly remains the truth. Nothing related to our agenda misses us. We see it everywhere, even where it isn't present. Our agendas don't escape us.'

'Or maybe we can't escape from our agendas!'

We caught some breath. But I still had a raging question. 'Can a situation affect people differently? and if it does.. what does it say of those who change?'

'"The same boiling water that softens a potato, hardens an egg."'

'Yeah. Exactly that.'

'Never underestimate the ability of life to teach two different people two different things using the same stroke. There's no shame in being softened by a circumstance which maybe hardens some others. Maybe at that time, someone needed a lesson in humility, and someone needed to toughen up. There is no shame in being an 'egg' or in being a 'potato'. As it is said, every new change is meant to teach, but what you learn depends on who you are. Remember, what the potato has the egg doesn't, and what the egg has the potato doesn't.'

We shared a quiet moment. The breeze was still on, and it helped me process her words. I sipped on my cup a few more times, and she said, 'Can I ask you something?' I gave her my attention, and she said, 'Do you ever feel that there is a need of someone around you? Someone who can bring the best in you? Someone who is willing to bear with us to the end?'

For once, I had the answer. 'I think, what we need is someone who will tear us apart. Limb by limb, sense by sense and cell by cell. Someone who will take the pains to break us down, to see what we truly contain. Someone who wants to see what hues and habits and traits we expose about us. Someone who won't flinch when our lighter and brighter hues are followed by our darker and bold ones. Someone who will keep on digging, beyond what wrath we lay on them, to find that one hidden jewel within us that truly defines who we are. Someone who will tear us apart, put a piece of themselves in us, and then sew us up again - whole, complete and reincarnated.'

She bid me the night and went to sleep. Left alone to my concoctions once again, I now thought about what I had learned today. As I finished my tea, I smiled. So basically, all I need to do is be myself. Or a better version than before. Someday, somewhere, today's tête-à-tête will help someone else by my words and hope so by hers as well.

Try to give something of you and try to keep something with you, in every situation or place you've been to. That way, you will always have something different to give everywhere and something new to take every time.

The Art and Grace of 'No'

Life is full of questions, and questions are a substantial aspect of life in general. The insomniac dilemma of should or should-nots; the severity of decision making; the worry of whether to move forward or not; the anxiety of the answer. Questions in life are like the water in a watermelon, comprising about 90 per cent of the entirety. Except, life doesn't derive its name from 'questions'.

Thankfully not — it's the apparent hiddenness yet omnipresence of questions affecting humankind which make them even more enticing to a mind. Usually, the appeal is after the solutions are sought and the answers found - before that the questions are different beasts; which need to be tackled, fought, defeated or overcome. It is after the 'beast' is down and you triumphantly put a foot over it that one thinks about the learnings and takes them into deeper consideration. That's when the lessons transform into philosophy. Let's just say, a philosopher is just a PTSD patient who's slain too many of the 'beasts', aka questions.

It is pretty evident then, that the dominion of a question depends on the answer. Upon further, easy introspection, one realises that the true power rests in a negative response - a quick positive answer to a question dents the question's potency to affect and teach. Clearly, the root of all things related to positive growth in a question comes out of a negative answer.

People generally say, 'learn to say "no"'. Which is fine, but more importantly I say, learn to accept a 'no'.

Lots of arguments have been made in support of saying no – it is not an easy task. You need to be sometimes blunt, while you need to be crafty on the other times. It is about staying true to yourself and being honest – either brutally or subtly.

However, if you learn to say 'no' to protect yourself, you must also accept a 'no' to protect others around you. If it is an art to say 'no', it is very gracious to accept a 'no'.

A no is a no, however, skilfully wrapped and presented. A blunt no may hit you like a dagger through you, a subtle one will pierce itself slowly and agonizingly the more time you give it to seep in. A 'no' is never easy to handle – even if you expect it; the actuality of it is still difficult to deal with. It is our habits, to visualise a 'yes' and build around it in our sweet paracosms. That little high is one of the best feelings around – a smile etched on the face, a happy endeavour throughout the day. The extra levels of dopamine can induce newfound traits – hitherto unsuspected patience and acceptance as such. The future is planned based on a decision not in our hands. And then, the 'no' comes and it shatters the mirage.

Sometimes, a pessimistic soul can see through the mirage and can prepare to lessen the blow. The soul then haughtily claims itself to be 'realistic', not pessimistic. It berates itself and others with "What did I tell you?" and "What else did you think was going to happen?"

Here, then, comes the part where the 'protecting others' concept comes through. Naturally, after a negative response one considers the type, reason and scope of it. "What type of 'no' was it? Was it a 'not yet' type of 'no'? Or was it a 'never, ever' kind of no? Or was it plain ignorance? Maybe it was a forced 'no'?" One tends to overthink on it. The more you think, the more obsessed you become. The more obsessed you become, the more you have the potential to ruin things. Similarly with the reasons, and the scope. "Can I convince them if I try again? Should I try again? If I try hard enough, will it be a 'yes'?" I've learnt to accept the finality of a 'no'. It is crucial to understand that the 'no' pings, but pestering further and pushing on is not going to change things. Nine out of ten times it will create more trouble for them – damaging their peace, their schedule, their monotone. From their disturbance, nothing great can stem for you. Thus, inherently, for your selfish regards, it is wise to let a 'no' be a 'no'.

What about you, then?

You see, sometimes it is about time. Or distance. Both play a huge role, literally and figuratively. A person far off maybe 'just a text away', disregarding the effect of time needed to reach them, but the actual distance does matter. Nothing will ever equate to an earnestly spoken word, complimented by a pair of penetrating eyes which seep into the heart. However, at times, the text hits the mark, and the distance becomes a moot point, and the time spent becomes valuable.

It is then you must understand that not every yes is a victory and not every no is a loss.

Sometimes it is about peace in general – sometimes venting the question is almost the answer. Sometimes the question ceases to exist in its former stature the moment it leaves your lips. Sometimes, the question doesn't exist – it just is a weird manifestation of the overthinking epidemic rampant in our generation. And when it comes to a 'yes', you're never sure that the 'yes' you've got is what you needed. Sometimes you get a 'yes' when you needed a 'no'. Which isn't very ideal. Sometimes you think you need a 'yes' but you get an actually needed 'no'. Sometimes there's a gut feeling of peace, which suddenly sets in. And, as someone very wise told me, "There are two moments when that gut feeling serves right - when you know you've done your level best and it is worth it, or you've craved and had junk food."

So, there will be situations when a 'no' gives you peace. That is the dark beauty of a 'no'.

Not every 'no' is a pain.

Not every 'no' is a dagger.

It is all about peace.

Yes or no, may peace be upon you.

THE HALLOWED QUEST #1

It is under the greatest of tribulations that a man shapes into the self he ends at. I say ends 'at', because as long as he lives, he is on trial, and at times he may grow or shrink, but he is never the same.

The question is, then, which trials should be for whom? Why is it that grown men do not know the pain that an eight-year-old shrugs off? Why is it that someone is oblivious to a growth that someone has outgrown? Why is it that someone is sleepless and many others are weaving dreams? Why is it that for some, their gods are sleeping with their eyes open? And why do people without gods must look for salvation in people who escape from them in the name of god?

A little boy, too young to know but old enough to question; walks around the streets looking for someone. He may be very small for travel but was bold enough to explore. He was probably naive for trying to poke his nose, but was brave enough to prod his finger.

On his way, he walks past tens and thousands of people who from afar looked like they were coming towards him, but as they came closer he realised they had eyes for the horizon. Everyone seemed like going away from him if he looked back, and while the opposite view presented a momentary spark of hope, the thousands who walked past him made him understand no one was going to stay.

The boy had questions, which only multiplied every second. He had no ways of research except asking, for he was poor. He had no wise old man to ask because he was alone. And he had no time to contemplate his loneliness because he didn't have a roof.

Within that bustling street, he saw a man standing nearby, with his shoulder resting on a pole. The man looked brusque - bare-chested and well-cut, his torso gave him away as someone not to be meddled with. His loose lower garment was wrapped around his waist. While it looked a little odd, the boy presumed that it was pretty expensive - not by price but by value. The man had a strange greyish layer on his body as a baby rubbed with talcum powder. The man's long, bony face had a look of no-nonsense. His eyes had a flame of anger, which could fire up any second. His long, thick hair was plaited and mounted on his head like an inverted cone, with celestial ornaments decorating it. He looked like he was idly playing with a black rope in his hands. A triple spiked rod rested beside him.

The boy, apprehensive as he was, decided to approach him. He came closer and before he could call him, the man said aloud, "Yes?"

Startled, the boy asked warily, "Um, how did you know.."

"That you were coming? I've been keeping an eye on you since long, boy."

"What? How?"

"I have ways," the man said, without looking up from his toy. "Anyway, what do you want?" he asked.

"Can I ask you something?"

"Is it something foolish?"

"I don't think so."

"Then ask away."

The boy took some time to frame it properly. Despite all that commotion around him, he found himself alone with the man, as if they were on a mountain top - away from all things worrisome. The man had still not looked up from his past-time towards him, but the boy could somehow feel his gaze on him. The boy felt a pressure unlike any he ever knew. He felt like his question could be the most important words to ever come out of his mouth. Out of a thousand things in his mind, he ended up with something he didn't perceive to be that important. He gulped, and said, "Who are these people, and why don't they stop?"

The man stopped fiddling with his toy. Scared, the boy hastily stepped back and was about to apologize when the man spoke.

"They're a herd," he said with disdain. "Dolts who think they're each the sayers of right things. Each believes that their judgement is impeccable, and their decisions are flawless."

"But, if they say the right things, their judgement is impeccable, and their decisions are flawless, how can they be the part of a herd?" The boy asked.

"That's because what they say, judge and decide aren't their thoughts, judgements and decisions."

The boy looked about. None of the walking folk cared to even look at them - a shabby man and mere child was nothing to waste time on. They all looked focused, and while some did frown, none betrayed any steps they were taking.

"Whose orders are they following?"

"They may not be orders boy. There are many different ways to get people to do your bidding," the man said with a tone of knowingness.

"Then? What are they following?"

"Some are following rituals. Some norms. Some are following trends while some are just following the guy in front."

"Where are they going?"

"Honestly, I don't know. I don't bother myself with where they want to go. For me, they are all going to one place."

The boy frowned. "And that place is?"

"Death and destruction."

"Oh," the boy paused. "But isn't that an obvious end? Like, everyone is going there isn't it?"

The man looked at the boy for the first time.

"Perhaps you only heard half of what I said. Yes, everyone is going to die, but not everyone will be destroyed."

"But why destroy them? Who will destroy them?"

"Not who will - what will."

"What..will?" The boy asked hesitatingly.

"Let's see.. that man in the suit will be destroyed by his arrogance. That lady will be destroyed by vanity. That old lady over there will be destroyed by regret, and that child - poor one - will be destroyed by his parents. The parents, in turn, will be destroyed by ignorance. That restless runner will be destroyed by greed, and that girl will be destroyed by ego. Some will perish to lust, while some will perish to rage. Some will succumb to revenge and many will be shredded by envy."

Stunned, the boy looked back in horror. "H-how do you know? And will each be destroyed due to this?"

The man ignored the first question. "No, these people getting destroyed don't concern me much. It's folks like that one.." he looked far into the crowd, beyond what was visible to the boy.

"It's idiots like him that lead to bigger, much bigger destruction." The man seemed like he was talking to himself. "Not only destroying himself but others around him. In the hundreds. Thousands." The man's eyes had a fire raging, as he gripped his toy tighter than ever.

The boy was genuinely terrified now, but the incoming education kept him going. "W-hat will happen to him? And to those who are destroyed?"

The man seemed to pop out of his reverie. "If you destroy yourself, then it's a simple thing. You die knowing what you've done. Your death, along with your life, will be a waste. If you are destroyed by someone, then it's difficult, for your death will still be an incomplete end, something among the realms of could have beens and should have beens. In that case, your death is futile, but your life, unfortunately, is still a waste. But if you destroy other's lives before-" the man looked directly into the boy's eyes, "let's say someone catches up, then your death will be a spectacle and your life will be a lesson."

The man's toy suddenly sprang into life and slithered onto the boy's feet. The boy, captivated by the man's eyes, had no idea about it. He still had the courage to prod further.

"So there's a lesson in death?" he asked meekly.

"Depends on what you do."

"But what if I am not destroyed before I die?"

The man's eyes softened – they were almost kind now. "Then we will meet again, as friends." He extended his hand and the snake slithered onto his hand, and slowly wrung around his neck. "Now run along, little boy. My job here is done, and so is your time."

As he started walking away with the triple spiked rod, the boy's eyes followed his footsteps, until he realised he had one last question, which he shouted out loud, "At least tell me who are you?"

The man turned and smiled. It was the most beautiful smile the boy had ever seen. The man did not answer, but kept on walking, slowly fading away into the horizon.

The Hallowed Quest #2

Why is it that throughout the history of man, he has struggled to come to terms with a sense of isolation? Why is it, that the idea of being alone has been associated with, or even birthed dark and negative condiments; ruining the flavour of life?

I do not see an absolute bad in being alone, nor do I see any absolute pleasure in the other end of the spectrum. Why is it, that the companionship of one person is often enough to make you forget the need of anyone else? Why does, often, within hordes of people my only company is silence and paradoxically, the noise of my own thoughts? Why is it that the daily trudge is a pain but with the right person even the longest of travels have no effect on your feet? Why does, then, time fly and stops at the same time with that one companion?

The boy walked on, occasionally glancing backwards. He could not forget the image of the man on his mind, it was etched there like notches made by the persistence of flowing water on a rock. He still questioned whether he did actually have the conversation he thought he did, for the man did not look real.

No, he didn't think the man wasn't real because he was dressed oddly, or because he had strange pets and tools. The man radiated power, something much beyond knowledge and wisdom. The man emitted wrath, and despite it not being meant for the boy, he was still afraid and wary of it.

As he navigated the stream of flowing bodies, he asked himself, whether he had ever led to destruction. Destruction of what or whom, he could not place, and he decided that since he couldn't recall anything, he was innocent. That being said, he was now apprehensive of being destroyed - he still wanted to meet that man again, positively as friends.

Before he could ruminate more, he was distracted by a mild light just ahead of him, onto his right. The light seemed to come from a small alley, which was covered with curtains. The wind would move the curtains, and the light would dance on the people walking past. But they might as well be blind, he realised again. A few people even tried to jump out of the light's path.

The boy went in to investigate.

He timidly pulled apart the curtains and peeked inside. Behind the curtains was an incredible room, decorated with heavy pieces of cloth and art. The floor was soft and plush, and a red carpet led to two elegant and regal thrones. The thrones were made of gold, with velvet and silk laded around it. On the left throne sat a man, with both his arms on the side rest, shoulders broad, chest out and back straight. The man was dressed like a king, with ornaments and heavily embroidered clothes, but what gave it away was the large crown on his head. Along with that, however, he also wore a frown on his forehead; and a conflicting expression on his face. The other throne, however, was empty.

The man saw the boy peek in and immediately ordered him in. His voice was strong, yet was mild and calm. His order was probably as polite as an order can be, but there was a measure of finality in his voice which meant it was supposed to be completed, no matter what.

As the boy walked in, he felt calm. He felt his anxiousness vanish, his torments gone for the while. He felt safe. As he slowly walked ahead, the man smiled and encouraged him to come closer.

When the boy finally reached the foot of the throne, he stood there perplexed. Sure he had heard of kings and their magnanimity, but he had also known them to be brash as well. He figured he should acknowledge the man in some way, so he bowed down. As he got back up, he looked at the man. The man wore a smile so real, the boy questioned if he had ever seen a smile that warm.

The boy stuttered, "Your – your highness -"

"What brings you here, child?"

"I.. don't know. I saw the curtain and was curious."

"Well, that is a good reason to be here. Settle down, and let's talk."

The boy sat on the floor and made himself comfortable. He didn't know what to say, but as usual, he had questions. And since his earlier endeavour with the man with the snake, he felt he can now ask questions. Despite a multitude of previous questions, it was the most recent one that came out of his mouth.

"If I can ask, sir, how does one not get destroyed?"

"By staying true."

"True to what, sir?"

"True to yourself, and true to the basic principles of the cosmos."

"Cosmos? What are those principles?"

The man took a deep breath. "The world, child, is a huge quagmire, and to navigate it there are certain set rules and boundaries by which an ideal man must live. These are the principles along which life should be lived."

"And these rules," the boy mused, "what happens if you don't follow these rules?"

"Destruction, like you asked. Damage, loss, pain. There is no circumventing these rules. The position of man is so crucial in the universe that on his shoulders rests a lot of things, and if he isn't perfect, society transcends into chaos - mind-numbing chaos. If people feign these boundaries but disregard it in reality," the man scowled, "I harbour no respect for them."

"So these people out there - "the boy pointed behind him, "are they following the rules?"

The smile vanished off the man's face. He sighed, "I'm afraid not."

"So they'll die and then are destroyed?"

"You don't have to die to be destroyed, son," the man said, his voice letting away a hint of sadness. "Sometimes destruction sets upon your path while you're very much alive, and swallows you whole."

The boy moved to sit on his knees and looked back, "So, many of those people are already destroyed?"

The man nodded.

"They don't look like they're destroyed," the boy said honestly.

"That is the pain about being destroyed while alive," the man said softly, "you can never really know who is destroyed. Destruction grasps you from within, gnaws you out, and the pain can be eternally tormenting." "In fact," his voice dangerously soft now, "it is often the invisible destruction which is the biggest of reasons society has become into a perpetual cascade of inflicted destruction. People seeking the same punishment for someone else even if their fate was caused by different and wrong circumstances," the man finished, his voice dark.

The boy noticed that the man had dug his nails into the cushions of his throne's armrests, and his eyes had pain which the boy couldn't place. For what it was worth, what could a regal king like him have pain about? Lost in his reverie, the boy looked at the empty throne. He wondered who it was for, but the king looked irked, so he decided not to ask.

"So, um, sir? If you follow all the rules you won't be destroyed?" he braved with another question anyway.

The man didn't answer. Almost as if in a painful reflex, he glanced wistfully at the empty throne and looked at the boy. The boy, for a fleeting moment, thought the man's eyes were wet, but as he blinked and looked again, they were normal.

"Sir... if I may ask, that other throne – "

"Wait, son. There are some things I cannot say as a king, and as an upholder of those rules. Pardon me."

He got up promptly and walked away briskly behind the throne. The boy didn't follow his path, and looked around, trying to amuse himself. Before he knew it, the man was back and had put a hand on the boy's shoulder.

The boy gasped. The man had completely changed. He was barechested, and his well-chiselled torso was glowing. He wore an orange flowing clothing below his waist, a necklace of heavy brown beads, and his long hair was tied up into a bun. On his shoulder, he had a bow, and a quiver of arrows was tied to his back. A solitary, naked sword hung from his hips. He looked happier than before, and the almost permanent frown on his face was gone.

"That other throne, son, belongs to my wife. I have always followed the rules of the cosmos throughout my life, and they have aided me pretty well most of the times. However, following those rules has taken from me, my love and my kids," he said, sitting down beside the boy.

"So the rules.. can also destroy you?" the boy asked, the epiphany putting many pieces together.

"Yes. There is no absolute way to be happy, I now see. Selflessness and a little self-care, both are necessary. To give and also, at times, receive a little, both are needed. Those rules and boundaries... I won't say are meant to be broken, but pushed for sure, particularly as time pushes humanity further and further. And also, if required, abolish some if they aren't pertinent anymore. The one way to be happy is probably to not have any remorse and regrets. If you do have them, then for your own sake, try to be at peace with them."

The boy looked at the man. His face had a happy determination which warmed the boy from within. "It is important to be happy," he blurts out and looked at the man. The man smiled, his truest, broadest smile yet, and affectionately nodded.

They both got up. "Let's go," the man said.

"Where?" the boy asked.

"Along the road, for a while. And then we will go our different ways."

"You're going to get your wife back, aren't you?" the boy asked excitedly.

"Yes," the man looked equally excited.

"Are you sure you can do it alone? Do you need help? Can I help?"

The man laughed as he held his hand and they started walking.

"Don't worry child, I've done it before."

Alone and Aloof

There was a god in front of us.

There were people behind me.

The temple bells were clanging.

The aarti drums were banging.

It was chaotic for me, and within that chaos, I wondered how many could find solace. It was a question I ask myself about mankind often - how can loudness and thundery beats make people find themselves, instead of tranquillity and peace. Then again, people as an entity has always confused me, and the more fragmented it becomes, the more confusing it gets.

But for once, the chaos was not affecting me. Nor was the fact that a temple isn't the place most people who know me would expect me to be. But most people who know me don't really 'know' me, and since they don't, they do not have the slightest idea about the lengths I could go for love, and heights I could reach with it. And that is good, in a way, as then they wouldn't have to deal with my shortcomings of self loathe and the lows I can sink to when I am not 'okay'.

Nothing affected me there, in an environment which is a guaranteed migraine trigger for me, because I wasn't alone. Not in the figurative sense this time, I was genuinely not alone.

I looked to my right, and the noise drowned out, the people vanished, and the heat wafted away.

Her head was bowed, covered with her pallu. Strands of hair swivelled out of that cover onto the side of her face, and she may not accept it, but I had a hunch she let it stay out cause she knew how much I loved it. Her eyes were closed – not tightly, nor pretentiously – but firmly, with conviction. Her chin rested lightly on her hands clasped in front of her chest. Her lips were moving, whispering the words of the aarti which I could not hear. The threads on her wrist stood out, and her earrings swayed every time she adjusted her head.

There may have been a god in front of me, and she might have been praying to the same god, but I was looking at a Goddess, no less.

It was then I realised how valuable it is to have someone who can make you do things you do not intently want to do, not because of threat or the fear of repercussions, but rather due to a belief of trust in tolerance. No one was so far able to extort me into a temple before, but she got me there nevertheless. I prefer to be revered rather than feared and to be in positive demand rather than remand. God, for me, has always been someone who is feared, and that curiosity made me seek flaws. God's flaws.

God may judge me but the weight of his sins outweigh mine.

I love the idea of god's infallibility. Man decided he wasn't good enough, or perfect enough, so he framed the idea of a being (or plural) in his image of perfection. That's fine, by the way. I have a question about the notion that when man realised that he wasn't perfect, the thought process moved towards, 'but someone has to be!' And later, more reasonable school of thought popped up that asked, 'eh, but who is?' Unfortunately, as man realised the onsight into a grey area, his insight towards it became of exploitation, rather than adherence.

God is supposed to be perfect. God is someone who doesn't make mistakes but is often rumoured to do wrong to ensure a greater right. A smaller wrong done ensures a bigger right, and whatever collateral loss the wrong may induce, is merely a price. Because right and wrong, probably, is easier to determine thanks to omnipresence and knowledge, rather than being in the mix, suffering the dilemmas and conundrums at the ground level. It's his bird's-eye view which may ensure what's right and what's wrong, apparently, and thus he stays aloof. Far, far away, silent, and quiet.

God made man in his own image, they say, and that has always been true. Quite like god, Man isn't bothered with the cacophony that emits from the stage of his life – as long as he has a reason to put his own music on. Man, quite like god, likes to stay away, far and quiet. Aloof, until things corner him – and when he is cornered, he cannot fight; for god didn't make him in an animal's image which can fight, but in his own, which makes haste and thus seeks aid, only to realise that he is the reflection of someone aloof, far, far away.

Some men, thus, never actually bothered upon seeing the events around them, and began exploiting the idea that they thought that god was perfect – and god became incitor-in-chief. Others began exploiting the fact that nobody is perfect – certainly not someone who's super powerful but quite aloof – and then god became nothing more than a reference; or an idiom.

They say knowledge is power, and maybe the power god holds in is not the power to change things, but the knowledge that he cannot change things. Changing things requires extensive knowledge of contexts and nuances, something a bird's-eye view does provide. The more he knows, the more grey areas arise, and the more complex the solution gets, eventually raising the workload. The more he sees the more he knows and the more responsibility it raises on him; isn't he who started it all? Quite like a student who has a lot to submit does nothing, as he is overwhelmed, God does nothing as well, cause he knows it's hopeless.

God stays aloof because even he is terrified of what he has created.

But thank god, literally, that he merely made man in his image and not a true replica, for some men do see the micro view; the worm's-eye view, and try to change things. One thing at a time, sowing hope, and reaping despair; burning bright only to be dissolved into the darkness. And what do they get in return? They get eaten up, swallowed by men in god's image. But the worst thing they get in return is a forlorn path to trudge, to reap hope and shine bright eventually - and be ironically called godlike.

To become god is the most forsaken honour of all.

She opened her eyes and caught me looking at her. She sighed and beckoned the priest carrying the holy fire towards us. The priest gave blessings to her and asked me to pray to the fire. I politely refused and smiled; only for the time to come to a standstill again.

I saw the unholy fire of blasphemy in the priest's eyes, for he thought no one was perfect bar god, and to refute god was to seek war. I realised I was alone, and the gods, the god people and the godless wanted me, and I smiled. It would have been better if man had made god in his own image.

If god chooses to be my enemy, I'll live like I always have, and fight as I've never before.

Sorry if I'm Sorry

Apologising is one of the basic manners taught to children in school, told to be used frequently, and advised to be taken in unconditionally. And yet, despite these clear instructions, apologies remain a murky process and endeavour for many.

Today I realised something about apologies.

It's that most people aren't afraid to apologise. The tendency to get back to normalcy and clear any kind of guilt or conscience is in everyone. And in that process, most people are willing to let go the amount and degrees of wrong that they experienced. They're even willing to let go their hurt in the entire melange and acquiesce to a neutral ground.

What people are wary of, I've found, is the idea of apologising as a negotiation tactic. The notion that an apology is the base of any hope of reconciliation, and it has to come from the other party. Here it becomes a tool to both, fuel and satisfy the ego, and when an apology is shaped as a tool, it ceases to become a route towards peace. In such a scenario it becomes a piece of weight in the scale of the relationship, and the one receiving said apology has his side heavier. It becomes an imbalanced relation, wherein if needed, the apology tool can be reused to win further arguments and even, shame the apologiser down the line for something he or she has already apologised for.

Apologies aren't meant to be something that is used. They are, etymologically and in utopian practice, a genuine expression of something that one believes will resolve matters. Apologies are said when the sayer believes in the relationship more than the feud, but the moment one is demanded, it loses all value and becomes a cosmetic string of words; which neither provides peace, neither a similar resuming of relationship.

Another thing that happens, this one post an apology, that the one receiving an apology gains a morally higher ground – as if the apology was a souvenir of victory in war; and that receiving an apology means they are vindicated and entitled to be absolved. It's sad that people act like they've won the argument, received some sort of superiority over the other - be in subjectively factual, hierarchical or moral - and enter a sense of faux entitled victimhood that cynically and ironically avoids introspection on their actions, words and flaws.

And due to this reason, we have the notion of the "value of sorry". When such an event takes place, wherein the receiver of the apology uses the apology as a stepping stone to climb over the apologiser, the apology loses its intended intention, aim and purpose; thus losing its value. Apologies are meant to break down the walls in between two parties, and either throw the rubble away or use them to protect the relationship from similar fallouts. Never, ever was the act of apologising supposed to be an act of conceding defeat or loss.

"Sorry", if said a lot, says a lot about the person and their need for inner peace. The aim of sorry being a manner taught to kids was to teach them right and wrong, and the development of the autonomy of one's moral compass. "Sorry", if received a lot, says a lot about the person's need for outer gratification. And that is the complete betrayal of the autonomy of a human's moral compass.

Sympathy comes along when you have a clear idea of right and wrong. Empathy comes when you realise the massive grey area in between.

PERSONAL

The Fallible Dependency

The days batter away, and the nights scamper from sleep. Twisting and turning, I question every nuanced alternate possibility, try to foresee each and every of its forthcoming repercussions; only to encounter a blocked road in both directions. Frustrated, I get up, storm into the gallery where mother nature was all guns blazing.

My queries were not the usual questions of career, family, love or lust. They weren't completely unique either, except for the fact that neither could I formulate them nor could anyone understand them. They were paradoxical, oxymoronic and confusing.

"*Live on the basis of what you see, not on the basis of what you're shown,*" a wise voice once told me. But I had no idea how to interpret that. Am I seeing wrong or people are not what they show to be? It was until later, that is, years and experiences later that I realised that people wear masks not to hide, but to show what they really are. That was when I let it go, left all expectations and care behind. I forgot what it was to depend on someone emotionally, to let someone else's wishes take over my decisions, and to compromise things for people close to me. I stopped appointing people as my pillars, stopped depending on them and taking their support.

Little did I know that all I had done is take out a bird from the heart of its cage. Now I needed to remove the cage from it's heart.

I took on a life of desolate carelessness. Which I mistook for being carefree. I adopted the crude, which made me rude. I rejected my own feelings, trampled others', and quashed my whinging conscience. I adopted a life of extreme self-importance, with no respect for others. One where I was at the peak of my self-righteousness. One where no one was a priority, no one important enough for me to lose my sleep for.

Why then, did I fail to sleep peacefully each night?

Someone once wrote that it is necessary to share your love to whom you love, because you never know when you may get hit by a bus. That it is beautiful to be desperate in need of someone's love. Someone encouraged people to be straightforward, to splash out your feeling and bombard your emotions.

But it doesn't work.

I used to love being horribly straightforward. I used to love sending texts to people who were important to me. I used to be reckless, one who used to jump into a storm without worrying about getting drenched.

I did not think about getting hit by a bus. I worried about them getting hit by a bus. I never worried about death - sure life is short but it's never really my trouble if my life is short. It's always others who are near me who live on to repent my short life. I used to worry about people leaving me forever, those I cared about, those I loved, those who were a pillar to me.

There is no beauty in desperation. It's a mirage, and if desperation isn't dealt with sanity and caution it often leads to desolation. The problem with desperation isn't your need, but your need for that need to be fulfilled.

But there lies the problem. Straightforwardness and reckless displays of your feels only leave you exposed. The world is in a trance of wishful, pure love, and your expressions of love are crude wake up calls to them. Simply because you, quite often, aren't the reason for their trance. I often felt low and fearing loneliness, about how maybe there will be no one to text to, and then share that text to my loved ones. It was naive, to think of people and want to feel them, touch them and understand them if they do not want to be felt, touched or understood. That desperation is beautiful to the sender - you are after all sending your love.

I've sent love. And I've learned things. Love isn't to be sent, broadcasted, or even packaged. Because I did think of my loved ones leaving me forever - I just contemplated the wrong type of forever.

But it teaches you. Pillars that fall teach you to stand up on your feet, and if I needed crushing to grow, so be it. I do hope an individual's desperation is marched by someone else's desperation because, for someone who was told to not be so desperate, it ends and leaves an out of control mind that demands control.

I do not know what I am now. Somewhere between hopeless and a ray of hope.

I walk back to my bed and try to sleep again. I battle with my sheets to find the right position to trap sleep. It is then the epiphany happened.

I realised that the worst of life's struggles are always towards the end of your biggest battles, at the end of the long day, and it is at times only a matter of finding the proper position of true comfort.

What Goes Around, Comes Around

When I was a little child and would come home crying from the playground; complaining that I had been bullied and robbed of my fair chances at play, my mother would often say, "Happens, son. One day, things will come around."

Mankind, in general, has been obsessed with questions many species probably never even considered. Not satisfied with the recent past, civilizations and societies have focused and devised theories concerning and trying to put together the melange of ancient justice, historical learnings and a tool for futuristic hope – often named '*Karma*'. The idea of everyone being accountable for their deeds or the notion that a hypothetical account of one's actions – both positive and negative – exists and reward and/or justice will be served has seen people endure, tolerate and last in times of adversity. Millions throughout history have set examples of fortitude resting on the hope of eventual avenging. However, no one really has an idea as to how and when the sceptre of *Karma* shall wield.. just that it will. Things will come around.

I never really understood the concept of sitting down and letting things fall into place. A crude observation of my surroundings led me to the quick realisation that no magic hand will drive my work towards completion and no imagined audience will applaud me for a job I have never done. Then why was I taught to let go of things that inconvenienced me gravely; told to forget the deeds that wounded me and erase the words that hurt me? If I had to strive for my happiness, why not do that with setting things right and burying the bones of vicious memories? Why must *Karma* be the hero to bring me my justice? How does *Karma* even work? If we accept anything we encounter, hear or suffer as a consequence of *Karma*, does that mean I can go about being impertinent and shallow and defend myself saying, "I'm just laying out your *Karma* for you?" Why must I wait for someone, somewhere to fight my battles and give me my redemption? Why must I sit doing nothing and wait for things to come around?

Funny thing is, no one has a definite answer as to within what time period things will come around. The sceptre of Karma may brandish it's judgement immediately, posthumously, or never at all! But one thing is for sure, they tell me. Things will come around, either directly or boomeranging back. You just have to wait and.. wait? The logistics are pretty bad... wouldn't it be great if there were instant reactions? If only Isaac Newton's third law could have been more time specific. How many times have I wanted things to come around quickly, and I am still waiting...

I wanted the sceptre of *Karma* to wield when my efforts were not rewarded when the deserving winner lost out to the opportunistic participant. I wanted it to wield when I wanted my worth but never received any. *Karma* must have been busy, or my worth was not as I expected it to be.. but then, who decided the credentials and rewards? Who seeped in a strand of hope - the hope of a fair judgement - into a system full of injustice? Why is it entirely plausible for someone to buy the rewards without hard work and people just accept it as another crack in this fragile world we live in? But I let it go, this shall pass. One day, I'll get my reward. Things will come around.

I wanted it to wield when I was left bereft of the friendly hands on my shoulders when people close to me were 'stolen'. Whisperers exist in the shadows to lay their eggs in the nests of foreign minds, and they sit on it until the time is ripe for them to hatch and ruin what was once a thriving relationship. Where was *Karma* when I forgave tens of mistakes but wasn't forgiven for one? Where was *Karma* when truth found impregnable barriers of lies? Where was *Karma* when I saw pictures with my 'friends' being merry without me and felt pangs and pangs of shock? But I moved on. Someday, someone will stay. Things will come around.

I wanted it to wield when the moment I dared to dream, some cynic would uproot my hope. When my ambitions were 'preposterous' and others' were bred upon. When I never got the opportunity to spread my wings as they were trimmed before I could realise they were built for a long flight, was *Karma* busy sipping coffee and chuckling? What about the dreams of hundreds crushed by thousands of cruel, narrow and bigoted minds? Or the aspirations of some which are uprooted by the shovels of jealousy and envy? *Karma* sure does love coffee. But I kept on striving. Things will come around.

I wanted it to wield when I wanted empathy but got only sympathy. When I got futile tips and hollow assurances about the future, stating, "You will be fine," when I needed just a silent shoulder to settle on? Answer me, Karma, why does no one seem to truly register or think about what is going on in a person's head/life in the present but always is keen on their past and their future? Why does everybody consider their present as prime and others' as unnecessary? But I detached myself from the dependency of others' opinions. Someday, I will show them how it's done. Only the grieved can understand the grieving. Things will surely come around.

I wanted it to wield when the love I gave never returned. Where was *Karma* when my care and feelings were crushed like a useless styrofoam cup, crumpled like an old newspaper and trashed into a bin? Where was *Karma* when I had no one to listen to me? When life itself had decided to shun me and the world was a dark, dark place? But I kept on rebuilding myself. Things will come around.

Oh, Karma, where art thou? When will things come around for me?

But wait!

What if *ALL MY EXPERIENCES* were actually things coming around?

Before I Sleep..

The world is a drama where the actors are mute, the viewers blind and the writers deaf. The stage is set, the monotone is set but the expectations aren't met. A sore thumb stands; watching, listening and blabbering in the world of the blind, deaf and mute. The day of life begins with promise and often ends with disillusion. The show begins at dawn and ends when you sleep, but before I sleep..

Before I sleep, I want to take a stand. I want to speak out. For it is speech that moulds, words that motivate, ideas that build, and emotions that make us alive. For years I was quite like my books, full of words yet silent as a forgotten metaphor. I want to give life back to the words that were glorified by the pen but left redundant by the typewriter. I want to ditch the greys and take a stand. I want to make decisions and have no regrets about them.

Before I sleep, I want to fight. I want it to be known that my strength was not my body, which made me altogether stronger than many. I want to remain a step ahead, a thought process further and to plan next. I want to be challenged because I know I am a flame and the challenges are nothing but gusts of wind to rouse me more. I want to wear my scars with pride and take my losses with respect and admiration. I want to be a warrior, a warrior of virtue.

Before I sleep, I want to win. I want to know what the world calls a triumph. I want to know what success means to the world. Because success makes the world know you and failure makes you know the world. I want to diversify into a hundred things but divert into none. I want to stop trying to write my name on water, but use the water to etch my name into stone. I want to grow, develop, and succeed so that I can say, 'I am what I am.'

Before I sleep, I want to make a difference. I am done standing still in an inferno of directionless travellers, watching time as it passes by. I am too tired of living each moment by simply counting it past – as if I had to repay the debt of time. I want to be the force of good change, a bringer of light into the darkest of times. I want to build, care, home and touch lives and be there, always. I want to be a change or a catalyst.

Before I sleep, I want to give. In a society where we recognise many but know none, I want strangers to find their faith in humanity. I want to give a child a dream and watch him go on and fulfil it. I want to give an old man hope that the world he lived in is in safe hands. I want to give opportunities to those who can't afford one, I want to give a platform to those who want to jump, I want to give wings to those who want to fly. I want to give my kids the opportunity to continue a mission I began – to give for the better, and to the deserving.

Before I sleep, I want to cleanse the cobwebs and the settled dust glued to the remnants of my life. I want to freshen my memory, rinse myself, and create a manuscript that'll transcend into time and memories – not for its length, but for its uniqueness. I want to clear the smog of the past so that I can let live my present and lick my lips over the future.

Before I sleep, I want to revive the conversations buried deep inside the sands of time. Those unsaid words, the suppressed feelings, the lost confessions. I want to rekindle the fires olden, for they're nobody's friend but are of everybody's need. The olden fires are the hottest, and they burn without charring. They can burn away the regrets and heartaches, and leave you at peace with your past. I want to accept my past so that I can move into my future without disquiet.

Before I sleep, I want to love and want love back. I want to know how many people I must lose to finally belong and to be loved. I want to break myself from the shackles of superficial love, of self-centred emotions and construed affections. For we're fickle characters, drunk on the desire of love, not love itself. I want to find the one without losing myself multiple times in the process. I want to embrace love to the extent that love falls in love with me.

Before I sleep, I want to be happy. I want to find my solace – be it books, sports, art, music, dance, or adrenaline. I want to find and build my temporary cocoon around things I love the most, so I know where to go to seek respite, seclusion and peace. I want to smile for the silliest reasons, laugh at the petty instances and enjoy every little thing life has to offer. I want to simply, be happy.

Before I sleep, I want to live. I want to have a heart to live in, a character to truly trust, and a mind to purely comprehend the mess my consciousness is. I want to live, love, be happy, and walk into the night with complete satisfaction. I want to be the life of someone, for loneliness isn't the lack of companionship in life, it is the lack of life in your companions. As the sun sets in the horizon, I want to raise my cup. But not yet, not yet. I want to convert my wants into needs. I will convert my wants into deeds. When I do sleep, do not weep, for I'll have taken all I could reap.

"The woods are lovely, dark and deep,

But I have promises to keep,

And miles to go before I sleep,

And miles to go before I sleep."

– Stanza from Robert Frost's poem,

Stopping by the Woods on a Snowy Evening

Beauty Beckons

The sun was about to rise, as her eyes opened. Waking up early was not a habit, but was her trait. She stretched and tried to make her asleep body awake, as the first rays of light penetrated the sky.

She watched as the sun rays pierced the night, slowly changing into hues of mild yellow, orange and red along with reflecting the natural blue. The cloud boundaries seemed to block the sea of red, orange and blue and looked like masses of puffy islands. Her fellows woke up sensing the dawn. She had taken to waking up a little early to witness the dawn of the dawn, for the most beautiful aspect of the beginning of the day was the first stroke of colour on the dark sky.

There's so much beauty, she pondered. The beauty within the sky, beneath the waters, above the land and within the being. Beauty spread around the world; in the oceans and plateaus, deserts and tundras, forests and fauna, and in the hills and mountains. Beauty, enough for everyone, but not entirely available to a single one. There's so much beauty that transcends past us when we are either ignoring it or enjoying some other variant of it. And then there is so much beauty we're never destined to see, simply because it just isn't our share of the pie. Yet, like how between finite there's always a possibility of the infinite, there's always a chance of surreal beauty underneath the mundane.

She spread her wings and took flight. The cool morning air breezed around her as she cut through the wind, and she took in the view. The concrete jungle, they call this. Tall buildings, shallow people. Huge homes, small hearts. A million ways of transport, yet disconnected. She turned towards a small hut on the outskirts, beside a little brook that rims up with water when it rains. The hut was almost in its own sweet world, adrift from the chaotic inferno that was the city; and vested into peace, tranquillity and it's own beauty.

She perched on the windowsill, where as usual there were grains laid out - rice, wheat, and so on. As she pecked and ate at peace, she gazed inside.

The old lady sat in her rocking chair, her head bowed, dozing. Despite her age, she never forgot to put out the grains for the little bird, and she was her companion in the mornings. Her face was lined and wrinkled extensively with a wet trail disappearing onto her cheeks. Her skin had loosened and hung over her bony body. Her long hair, grey with a few strands of black in colour, was tied into a long plait which ran down just below her shoulders. She wore a white dress, with her reading glasses tied around her neck by a black thread. She seemed to be holding a photo frame in her hands, with the photo on the up, wet with a few drops of tears on it. The photo showed a young, spectacularly beautiful lady, holding a baby and kissing it on its forehead. Her son, who went out to serve his country in war, went missing, and never returned home. She remembered her son, his beauty, the beauty of motherly love and the beauty of the memories that were etched into the photo.

She watched the lady, and ventured towards the brook, hoping to find some water. Unfortunately, it hadn't rained for days, and the brook had nought to offer but a glimpse at its bottom. The sun rays falling on the mud mildly cracked open the soil, but it still remained cool and moist and soft. Step on it, and you feel that the brook remembers it's gushy past, it remembers quenching the thirst of many. It remembers the colours it spread when its droplets touched the sun rays, it remembers the green it helped spread on the plains. The brook remembers it's beauty.

She saw a man approach the hut. He was the first visitor she had seen arrive at the hut, yet he seemed to walk towards the place with a strut and familiarity that intrigued her. He glanced by the windowsill and knocked on the door.

The knock on the door almost jerked the old lady up. Probably the mailman, or the young boy who lived nearby and aided her with the groceries and the bills. She set the photo on the table beside her chair, got up and slowly walked to open the door. As she did, a man stood in front of her, tall and strong.

'Yes?'

The man didn't answer, instead, he gazed hungrily at the old lady. His eyes took his fill of the old lady's face. Her voice ringed around his mind and brought out the scattered remains of his childhood memories. His face was a concoction of emotions – relief, happiness, tears and love. He couldn't stand anymore, and his mouth throatily blurt out,

'Ma!?'

The old lady was startled. She put on her glasses, and there he was. The son who had left for the motherland had returned to his mother. The son whom she had cradled and cared for, strived and caressed for had finally returned to her lap. The same hungry eyes, the crooked nose, the broad shoulders and the greasy voice. Tears began flowing down her cheeks, more freely than they ever did. She pulled him in, and hugged him tightly, just to make sure he was real and wasn't going anywhere. No words escaped her lips, yet the welps of joy and happiness along with the simultaneously flowing tears were a sight of beauty only the viewer can grasp, not express.

The weather seemed to feel the beauty and decided to grant it's own touch. The clouds darkened for the first time in days and a drizzle started to fall. The brook rejoiced as she took shelter under the window parapet. Soon, the brook began to fill up, and within no time it was brimming with water. The rain gradually stopped, the skies cleared, and the sun rays hit the brook and split into colours on the edges of its banks. The brook recalled it's glory, a glory which satisfied the thirsts of many and eyes of a few.

The mother and son sat, with the old lady on her rocking chair and the son at her feet. He had her hands in his, his head in her lap and his ears to her song. Once in a while, he would recollect a memory, and her mother would smile and laugh with a twinkle in her eyes. She looked as if she had gotten younger. And when she smiled, the entire surroundings stopped and stared for a while, because there was the beauty the world was once mad for, but now that beauty belonged only to her two children, her son and the little bird.

It was time to go back. As always, one has to return home. She took flight again and flew into the setting sun, which knew it's ablaze beauty, and beckoned for more. The sun remembers it's beauty of the dawn at dusk and promises more, for every dark night ends with dawn's beauty to the fore.

The Ugly Manling

The man snored, swaddled in the cradles of sleep. Morn was about to crack open, as was yet another day of warring. The sun soon rose, awash in its colours, dripping it's hues over the sore sky, with the night melting away. Rays sneaked in and onto the man's face, waking him as gently as a mother would.

As he was getting dressed, he couldn't help noticing what he saw every day. The mirror reflected back the jarring realities of himself. The dark, scarred face saw him back, smeared with red pimples. His lips were swollen always, and he made quite some jokes at that to amuse him. His eyes ran up to his forehead, above which hair had refused to grow since years. He liked whatever hair he did have, and refused to shave it clean. 'You look thrice your age,' those who were willing to talk told him. 'Ugly,' they called him behind his back.

He began walking on his path to work, as he did every day. No one had eyes for him, and those who managed a glance looked away as hastily as they could. People pointedly stayed away from his tracks. He walked in a cloud of gloom he didn't choose to have, and it rained sympathy and hostility he thought he didn't warrant.

He arrived at a crossing, which was an inferno of pedestrians and vehicles on their own ways. The women walked away briskly, adjusting their make-up and the men trod on, combing their hair in the process to look presentable. Within that maze of zig-zag motions of self-obsessed people, an old lady stood at a crossing on the road, patiently waiting to cross the road. She stood there, with her day at a standstill while the word continued to move around in its strenuous nature. He paused, wary. Looking around, he saw that nobody had the time to even notice this lady, forget helping her. For all his helpful tendencies, he was afraid. Instances had made him wary of reactions to himself, yet he decided to approach her.

In the world of busy beauty, the ugly man walked the old lady across the road.

As he approached his workplace, a stray dog leapt at him. Barking happily, the dog began licking his face. They made a queer sight; a stray dog playing with an ugly man on the side of the street, which made people stay away. What the posh thought was filthy and dirty, the living felt love in that. The dog didn't seem to find him ugly and lonely. They shared a bond deeper than anyone he had had with before, whether it be a part of his lunch or rushing to save him from kids who pelted stones at the dog. The dog, in return, kept an eye out for him every day, for once, making him feel welcome, somewhere.

In a world of indifference, the ugly man showed compassion.

Back from work, he saw a poor, homeless man on the footpath below his apartment. He rushed up, sought his old blanket and gave it to the poor man. The poor man got up, startled and tiredly afraid of another evacuation when he saw the kind smile and soothed. They shared tea until late into the night, the poor man and the ugly man.

In a world of stoic tolerance, the ugly man radiated kindness.

Beauty. It is a question, more than a state of art notion of philosophy. A question that was asked millions of years ago, a question that has been answered in different versions. But the truth remains, that we have always chosen the wrong answers to live by. The truth is that those who have never aid below the starry midnight sky have no idea what serene beauty is. The truth is that those who have never helped someone in need have no idea what the beauty of gratitude is. The fact remains that those who have never seen an old couple in each other's arms have no idea what the words, "I love you" mean. The fact remains that those who have never lived have no idea how beautiful is life, beyond the shades of mascara and beyond the notions of exterior attractiveness.

There is beauty in this world that is flowing. Ageing. And then there's a beauty that is stagnant. It is the same difference as it is between a flower and the woods - one a blush, the other a perennial bloom. Flowing beauties of the world wane; their definitions temporary. They are a shell, superficial and hollow. But within each shell lies something indelible and endless - something that will never cease; something that defies time like time has never been defied before. It happens so often, yet we think it has flown away. It's that ever enduring beauty that makes life worth living, that makes the work worth doing, which makes one love living.

To Dream A Dreamer's Dream

It is two thirty in the morning. I lay in my bed, wide awake, gazing at the ceiling. Another night ruined, adding to the countless hours of sleep already lost. It's almost as if sleep forgets to drape me in its cloak every night. Thoughts begin to pour in, noting the day ahead and the challenges ahead. Soon they will drift to the days past and the moments lost. Being a man of situational conformity, I let them do whatever they want to.

I try to deduce my lack of sleep. Science has it's answer, as do my family. None of them convinces me. As of, a scary thought hits me. What if I am afraid to sleep? What if, I am afraid to *dream*?

Sure, I had dreams. Elaborate and vivid dreams. Dreams that were crushed, dreams that never came into fruition. The child who saw those dreams was mocked by everyone, even it's elder self. The castles that were built in thin air, the worlds that were furnished in isolation and the experiences that were furbished conveniently; all vanished when reality stuck.

They say a dream is not something which you see at night, but something that doesn't let you sleep. I've found, more often, that it's the ghosts of the dreams dead and buried that don't allow you to sleep. They put you in a lucid trance, where you're neither fully awake nor fully asleep. They render you afraid to sleep, afraid to dream, afraid to take off into the pastures of your own excellence. They close the doors to the expeditious possibilities, and make you believe that flying is not for you, and tell you that risk is a damning concept of the unruly, wasted and lost. They tell you that there is a formula for everything and things are supposed to pan out in a manner. They teach you pragmatism as an inhibitor, not as an armour.

I embraced realism. I drilled it into myself that everything is planned, every action should have a definite reaction. I convinced myself that the world ran according to physics in every sense. I believed that the world was a program and each input has to have a definite output.

The world and it's inanimate segments may function that way, but it's soul; life and it's animate characters, work by no rules.

I get up, prepare myself a cup of tea. Might as well delve fully into this pond of solitude. While sipping on it, my solitude angel plays another twist, drives me into the memories of someone whose dreamer within was still intact, pure and going strong.

She talked about catching the clouds, planned to sail the winds and run with the rivers. She just wanted to do things. She wanted to take jumps without fearing the falls, wanted to swim against the tide, wanted to fall in love without being afraid of heartbreak, she wanted to add up all her days into a life, and as the sun goes down on her, she wanted to raise her cup in recognition of her life. She didn't live by any rules bar her own. And she needed no saviour.

I never really got the concept of strong women – or men, for that matter – not needing a 'saviour'. The way I see it, we all have our demons to fight, and a little help is always welcome. A saviour can be anyone, even someone who puts in that 0.1% required when you're exhausted totally, when you're about to drown very close to the shore. Being independent does not mean that you don't need help if it means something; it means that when you do need help, it's monstrous.

I wanted to sit with her on her journeys, hope to catch her when she eventually fell from the dizzying heights she scaled. But she never fell. She kept on scaling, she kept on dreaming, she kept on going away from the base where I was. Soon it so happened that I was losing sight of her. I tried my best, to get her back in sight and into safety. But she was beyond reach by now, and all I could do was to try and reduce our distance.

She made me lift off, taught me to cheat on my formulae and showed me how to dare to dream. She showed me how to revive the dead dreaming child within. At the cliff, at the end of her foray when I finally was in the same dream as she, I realised that it all is a matter of jumping in, and the view from the top is breathtaking. I was shown that it is worth living on the edge, for at the edge you get to experience things that are bouldered on at the centre.

But the cliff wasn't my domain. I wanted to get down. Back where I was comfortable. Back into the grasp of my formulae and programs. And I wanted her with me. I had dreamt the dreamer's dream.

She refused to get down.

"There are dreamers and there are realists in this world. You'd think the dreamers would find the dreamers, and the realists would find the realists, but more often than not, the opposite is true.

See, the dreamers need the realists to keep them from soaring too close to the sun.
And the realists? Well, without the dreamers, they might not ever get off the ground."

— Modern Family

Beginnings Till The End

She wasn't sure what was more out of the ordinary - the medicines or the cake.

The medicines have been her companion for a strong twenty months now. The pills and syrups along with the injections and other high doses now represent her life in its crude glory – a battle every day to survive. She popped in more medicines in a day than most do in months. The sudden diagnosis led to the beginning of a whole new way of life, adrift from a totally different life prior to it.

Then there was the cake, in the hospital. A small, modest one, with a tag of 'Happy Birthday' and a cherry on top. It was reminiscent of the better past, when she was a normal girl – studying, working and enjoying her life. It was almost like the disease was otherworldly, and her life span had been divided into two distinct timelines – Before Casualty and After Disease.

It reminded her of her father, who was a soldier on the borders; and whose life threatened to create a similar bifurcation. Every evening she would wait for his call, the lonely man thirsty for the voice of the apple of his eye. She was too young then, and the call only meant the few minutes when the father and the daughter were together, but as she grew up, she realised that the call was the daily reminder that her father was still alive, at least until the next call.

One day though, the call did come, but it wasn't him.

The dawn of the single parent in her mother, and the fatherless child in her made her grow up quicker than it was fair. But fair isn't how life is, she had understood that by now. It was supposed to be a new beginning, learning to work the unicycle when she was so used to the bicycle.

She wasn't really at terms with her new life when the disease struck. Her mother did come from a wealthy family and could afford her medications. But life was never going to be the same again.

She figured that life was a series of different beginnings till the end. Of all sorts. She wasn't sure about the endings, but she tried to focus on the beginnings. Much more optimism. Some beginnings were voluntary, while she never realised when some onsets occurred. Some made her feel happy and ecstatic and there were some which dampened things extensively. They began and continued until something else began, and what had begun was now water under the bridge.

Love had its own beginnings, when he showed up every day at her hospital bed. His charm could make her smile even felt she didn't feel like it, and often they talked into the night. But he became erratic, and when she actually began to look out for him she had to wistfully look away to the chair he would sit on. He fell in love with her quickly, and fell out of her love quicker. She took time to fall in love with him and is taking her time to fall out. She had underestimated his ability to fall in love, and he had underestimated her capacity to stay in it.

Another beginning then, to move on. There were times when sometimes all she needed was a shoulder, but all she got was a pillow. She began to find solace in art and poetry. She was told she was good, but she doubted herself. 'Self-doubt doesn't let you fly. Self-criticism, on the other hand, is the thread of the kite which keeps it from flying away, lost from view, but also allows you to reach new heights,' her father would often say. She went about sharing her work and marking her own improvements. She immersed herself in art and art responded to her whims. She kept on nagging herself, to improve, to build, to create. 'Nagging yourself is necessary. It will lead to a flicker, then into a flame and then into an inferno,' her father's voice echoed in her mind.

Yet, sometimes she would sit and wonder what she wanted from life. Was living on pills and counting her days out what she wanted? Was her aim only to survive? Or to make the max of whatever she had left? A dilemma of gargantuan proportions and she never had the answer. That scared her, it scared her so much that it almost scarred her. This time, her mother came to her rescue.

'Not knowing what you want from life is not the scariest thing, my child. The scariest thing is knowing what you want but not doing the required work to get that. The scariest thing is knowing what you want and can't have it. The scariest thing is knowing what you want and having not lived for it.

You have a blank canvas. You don't know what to paint on it, but that doesn't mean you'll never know. For some, it clicks at 18, for some at 25, for some at 40. It doesn't matter when you get to know what you want from life, but it is necessary to do your absolute best the moment you realize why you live.'

So she delved in. Fully. Determined to make her time worth it, focused on beginning her final chapter in the best way she could. 'Do something and people will look at you. Keep on doing things and they'll look up to you. Tell them you can do the things as well and they'll follow you,' her parents seemed to echo. She felt strength pouring in when she picked up the pen, her art and poetry touched hearts. She realised that the world needs introspection when all we do is investigation. She felt the power spinning at the tip of her pen, and the creativity hurling in her mind. She let it all out, sketch by sketch and prose by prose. She wanted to live beyond her lifespan, so she began to etch herself into minds and into hearts.

She felt as if she had the golden snitch in hand, and at the very end, life made sense.

"I open at the close."

- Harry Potter Series, J.K. Rowling

She cut the cake, with the mother smiling at her, holding back tears. 'You're a strong woman,' the daughter thought, with admiration. 'There's my strong girl,' the mother thought proudly.

She knew her father was looking on. Maybe, even awaiting her.

Who knows what new beginnings death has to offer?

The Lake Of Desire

The night was dark, the moon shy. The world was quiet after the entire day's noisy bustle. The cool wind ruffled the leaves of the trees, filling the air with a rustling noise. It was only fitting that the silent life could finally vent out its fury. Each leaf seemed to scream aloud in pique, with the wind determined to carry the message as far as it could. The ambient silence only amplified the ruckus, and the wind hissed along in consternation. The night was raging.

Sleep had managed to douse the potential listeners, but there was one listener, awake, on whom sleep had given up, or maybe he had given up on sleep. He was no stranger to this umbrage, he heard it every night, felt it every night. The night's rage was a part of his schedule, but tonight felt a little uneasy. The night seemed even more vexed than usual. He had learnt to live with the noise, even enjoy it now, after hours and hours of fright. He got to his nightly penance, a two-mile-long trudge on the jungle floor, barefoot.

The wind picked up, finally finding a listener. The wind roared and the trees swayed, and he tried to walk against the roar and bawl. The leaves shrieked even more loudly, surprised as every night with this man's obstinate ritual. Every night he would wage a war against their disquiet, face their wrath to trudge to a lake nobody else knows about. A lake they were supposed to be guardians of. A lake that no one knew about or had managed to reach. Except him.

His repeated success in managing the get past their fury only resented them further, and they tried harder each passing night to stop him. Tonight was the night he would be stopped in his tracks, tonight was when he would pay for his repetitive excursions against their will. Tonight was the night, when he would finally join them. Even the moon decided to show up, marvelling at the man's fight.

The man moved ahead, slowly but steadily, putting one firm foot forward at a time. The wind lashed against him, threatening to rip away every hair on his head and the skin off his skull. He never understood why the forces opposed him, all he did was go to the lake and look into its water and wait for dawn. Years ago, he had heard that the lake was magical, and it's still water could show you your deepest wishes, and if you desired them with absolute purity, it could even fulfil them. The water had shown him nothing but the pitch black of its seemingly bottomless self, and occasionally, if the moon decided to be friendly, his own tired old face.

Why then, did he go to the lake every night? Surely the magic was a hoax, the journey futile? But he still found himself taking on the guardians of the lake every night. He had no idea why he did that. He was devastatingly alone, devoid of a purpose in life until he had heard about this lake. He then made the lake his purpose, but after discovering it years ago, he still could not let go of it.

The wind had become a tempest, and the lower branches of the closely knit trees began swinging at him. It was when that happened he realized that he was close, almost too close, that the trees and the wind were trying desperate measures. It won't be long, like every night, that they would let him reach the lake in countenance.

He put his head ahead, and with one final push, moved into the clearing. All of a sudden the wind dropped and the noise settled. He had reached the centre of the storm. He fell onto the lake bank, tired than ever before. After catching his breath, he looked up, and let out a scream of shock.

There was no lake. The place was the same, he could have sworn, but where once the lake was, now was a barren piece of land. Bewildered, he looked around, trying to make sense of whatever was happening around him. Everything was the same, like every night, just the lake had vanished.

He walked towards the land where the lake once was, but wary. He now had confirmation that the lake was magic, but how and what did that magic do, he had no clue. He noticed a region marked by queer particles, like someone had murdered the lake and left a chalk trail around its body. As noisy as the shell of the lake area was, the core was eerily quiet.

He hesitatingly put a foot beyond the marking, and found it firm. He then closed his eyes in apprehension and put his second foot inside.

He gently opened his eyes after a few minutes and looked straight at a lady. He recognized her as the one he wanted dearly, but one he never had courage opening up to. He thought that this was his eternal desire. Before he could say a word, the lady changed appearance.

She now looked like his late mother, whom he hadn't seen for most of his life. Staggered, he froze, unable to think or move. He tried to move towards her, but his feet were lead. Tears streaming in his eyes, he stretched out a hand towards her...

The lady changed shape again. Now she was his sister. And again. Again, and again and again. Each time she took the form of someone who he wanted to be with and be for but couldn't. Then she started showing him his wishes, dead and unfulfilled.

She then showed him his failures. Each passing form made him writhe even more in agony. He tried to scream but no sound came out. He tried to run but couldn't move. He tried to close his eyes but he could still see things with his eyes closed.

He wept and wept, begging the lady to stop, wishing for death, wishing that he had never found the lake, wishing that the windstorm would have killed him. He writhed and cringed, tried to tear himself apart, pulled his hair our and gnashed his teeth in when finally it stopped.

He had no courage left, and lay on his back, exhausted and dying. Each form the lady showed had sucked the reason out of his life. With every form, the lady had snatched a hitherto unknown factor to him as to why he made the journey to the lake every night. Transformation by transformation, she had shown him what he truly desired - love, acceptance, and success. But that comes at a cost, he realised. Knowing what he desired truly meant that he was wishing to be reunited with his loved ones, in a place where all his wishes would be fulfilled and he would have the success he deserved. Little did he know, he desired death.

Now he knew why no living man had found the lake before. Now he knew why the wind and the trees didn't want him here. Everyone who found the lake had desires vested in the past, as reparations or regrets. The ones whose desires were held in the future had something or someone to live for. They needed no lake.

The lake *was* magic. It showed him his desires. And it also fulfilled them.

He felt the water beneath him, and could slowly feel it rising. He made no efforts to move. Instead, he smiled, truest one he had in years, and waited. Waited to drown and finally fulfil his desire.

He waited, to finally join the trees into warning any traveller searching for the lake into trying to live.

Who Art Thou?

The cool breeze ruffled our hair. The fading sunlight fell onto our faces, more like gentle rays than harsh beams. Looking up, you could see fiery orange between the dark greens of the canopy of the branches. We sat on the park bench, with our arms occasionally brushing against each other. The setting sun signified the end of our time together, and she decided to ask a question whose answer is more varied, elusive, and invisible than time.

"What sort of a person are you?"

I glanced at her. Her face was a mix of anxious and amused concentration. She knew perfectly well what she had asked, and how that simple question had the power to stir things up beneath the supple veil of consciousness.

I almost blurt out the kindergarten introduction I memorised years ago. Holding back, I tried to reform it into something a twenty-one-year-old would say. Before I could even form a couple of sentences, she clarified her question.

"Don't give me your introduction. This isn't an interview question."

Her eyes bored into mine, and I realised what she was asking for. She wasn't asking for my on paper qualifications which I had gained by roting lessons, she was asking for the lessons I had learnt by making grievous mistakes. She wasn't asking what I wanted to show the world, she was asking for what I knew I was.

So, what was I? Within the life story of eat, sleep, play, learn and repeat; where did my identity come in? Between in the search of societal validation, education and remuneration, where did my personality play a part? In my quest for gratuitous love, affection, friendship and acceptance, what did my nature influence?

Time slowed down, and my mind raced back into childhood.

I was the youngest, not only among my immediate but also among the extended family. There's something all youngest members of a nuclear family agree upon, we hold more responsibilities than people think, society perceives and get credit for. Add into it the fact that we're actually supposed to be absolved of accountability until a certain age catches up with us, and our lives begin to paint a picture of carefree beginnings escalating to careless adolescence. From there on begins a rocky path towards adulthood, marred with unexpected revelations and disappointments which don't really surprise anyone. And therein, I realised, my first building blocks were laid.

There was a child, forever in his elder sibling's shadow. Knowledge is often mistaken with academic flourishing, and it was no different for me. Whenever a general knowledge question was raised during family meets or guest talks, it was assumed by default that I never knew the answer. Until one fine day, there arose a question no one had the immediate answer to, and for once my laid back brain decided to have my back. The sheer incredulous reactions from my family gave me part satisfaction, part motivation. I made a conscious decision to stay ahead of the curve. That was me, striving to have no one take me lightly, and if they do, it's at their own risk.

I had realised early on that it was impossible to please everybody, so I decided that disappointing everyone equally wouldn't be a bad idea. Of course, that's horribly flawed, which I grasped only after I disappointed some more than it was warranted. But all in all, I learnt a very important lesson. It is important to disappoint people. It may not sound glorious or chivalrous, but keeping people - even close ones - on a higher pedestal than necessary has its repercussions, most notably on yourself. At times, disappointments act as a subtle reminder that the person in front of you is human, capable of making mistakes and has flaws. Disappointments often are the inaugural pickings of a stable work bond. But alas, modern people have no time for disappointments and mistakes, let alone bonds. Then there is me, looking for bonds and rapports in a world where egos and reputes are so fragile that they crack at the first kernel that hits them.

Have you ever closely observed the dew on the flowers in early winter mornings? It's a sight to behold. The drops seem to inflate the beauty of the flower. A famous poet once visualised the dew as the tears of the flower. When you look at it from that point of view, it paints a rather accurate picture of humanity - celebrating and enjoying someone else's pain. But it also points out that admiration and wonder come at the end of difficulties and pain. It is probably that sense of acceptance of challenges and difficulties that I have engraved onto my character, which makes me wait for times when I'm admired and esteemed. The wait isn't easy, but all I can and will do is to take on challenges and destroy them.

I tend to help people. That's a part of who I am. There's this saying in India, '**Do Good And Throw It Into The Sea**. (नेकी कर, दरिया मे डाल)' I often interpreted it as do good and forget about it, you don't need to remember it; in line with the famous Bhagavad Gita saying of karma and reward. However, very recently did I have a eureka moment when I figured out what exactly it means. Have you ever stood on the shore and thrown something into the sea? What happens after some time? ***IT COMES BACK***. The waves bring it back. The lighter the thing, the quicker it comes back. In the exact same way, small good deeds come back quicker than bigger ones. But then, shouldn't the bigger deeds have bigger and quicker rewards? There's a reason smaller good deeds have quicker returns. As my experience says, doing a hundred small good deeds is way more difficult than doing one big good thing. It's because doing small good deeds in regularity means that the propensity to help, work and build is ingrained in you and it has become your habit. You don't have to make a conscious decision to be good. There I am, just trying to be good.

To love is to bleed. It is as simple as that. It is very apt, then, that the flower of love is the rose. To pluck it and present it, you must thrust your hand into the thorny bush, bleed a little, but once you have the flower, you cut it's thorns so that it doesn't hurt your beloved. If that isn't an accurate representation of love, I don't know what else is. The cutting of the thorns off the stem of the rose also portrays that you may be beautiful, sweet smelling and blossoming, but you aren't ready to love and be loved in return until you cut those hurtful thorns off. Grow for love, but also trim yourself, for not every growth is positive. It is a lesson I learnt by scratching and bleeding many I love. Maybe I'll find someone who will tolerate all my remaining thorns. Maybe I will cut them all off. I don't know.

But then I have my demons. I'm opinionated. I'm not a sweet talker. Coarse. I put people in uncomfortable situations with my words. That leaves me alone at times. To the extent that I wish to yell out a challenge,

"No, you can't tolerate me. You cannot withstand me. I'm maybe too toxic. Too corrosive. Very bluntly sharp with my tongue. You can try to handle me, many tried to. Wear your safety gear. Do what it takes, then. Neutralise me. I am pH 1, are you pH 14?"

I need people. I admit. Stay with me. I'll deal with your rains, your sunlight and your storms. Just not your absence.

I looked at her and smiled. The answer to that question isn't given, or said, or written.

'Find it out, will you?' I smirked.

Grow Up, Grow Old

"Kids think with their brains cracked wide open; becoming an adult, I've decided, is only a slow sewing shut."

— Jodi Picoult, My Sister's Keeper

The sun was going down, and it was getting dark really quick. I scrambled around the locality, frantically searching for her.

Where could she be? We had to be back home by now. It had been a long day.

I almost did not notice the children's park gate and had passed by it when I heard a solitary creak. I tracked back and peeped in to see her on the swing.

I went in, relieved and angry, walking towards the swing.

"Oi, what are you doing here!?" I exclaimed.

She looked at me with a mischievous smile on her face, "Come, sit on another swing with me."

I gaped at her. "Have you lost it? We need to leave, now!"

"Where to?" She smiled knowingly.

"Home!"

She took some time to respond. "I don't want to go home," she whispered.

I've been here before. This was going to take a long time. I heaved a huge sigh, and took the swing beside her.

"Why not?" I asked her.

"It's just boring," she said. "Wake up, Uni, work, go home and sleep. What about other things?"

"Other things like what?"

"Like just sitting on swings. Looking at the stars. Going for a long peaceful walk. Stuff for the heart, you know, not just for the schedule."

"There's no time," I said. "There's still a lot of work to be done, preparations to make, chores to finish."

She made a tch tch sound. "There's a lot of time, you just don't want to find it."

"What!?"

"What I mean is, learn to take a break."

"From what, for what?"

She looked at me and pushed away some locks of hair from her face. "From the monotone, for yourself."

"I'm fine with the monotone. It works well with me, and I have no qualms about it."

"Okay, then tell me; when was the last time you relaxed, picked up a book and read for hours at once?"

That hit me like a thousand slaps. It was true, I hadn't read in months. Maybe even for more than a year. I had no idea how it came to this, when once upon a time I used to read a book per week. What troubled me was the fact that I didn't even realize that I missed reading, and her reminder brought back all the collective yearning back, with interest.

"Yeah, okay. I miss reading."

"I know you," she said. "You love what you do. And you also love to be doing something always. You like to be busy,

busy enough to maybe keep your mind off things that you may not want it to ponder about. And you're even prepared to let go of other things for that, even if they're other things you love doing too."

I was lost for words but still tried to say something. "Yes, but –"

"And that's a good thing," she cut me off. "People wish to be where you are at the moment. I am just telling you to spare some time from your week for your heart and soul. Things that replenish you. Rejuvenate you. Things that you still wish you were paid to do. Things that harbour the petty joys and silly laughs. Things that, essentially, charge your batteries."

"You never get enough of them," I said with quintessential stubbornness. "Such activities are like a swamp or a quicksand. They pull you in, you lose track of time and perspective."

"What perspective?" She arched an eyebrow.

"The perspective of responsibility. Of impending work. Slack off and you fall behind, and the workload increases and increases, and you start lagging behind." I said with definitive finality, as if there was no sounder logic than this.

She shrugged. "Courts function every day with hundreds of pending cases. Countries splash around while still being in millions of debt. Here's the harsh truth, the world functions exactly the same even if you make some mistake. You're running breathlessly at the moment. There's a certain amount of adrenaline about your passion, no doubt. But this isn't sustainable. You can't go on like this."

"So what do you suggest? I stop doing everything I do and start fooling around, as no good losers do?" I blurted, a little irritated.

"I'm not asking you to stop. I'm asking you to pause from time to time. Take a deep breath. Listen to some of your favourite songs. Go for a short coffee break and stare into the sky from your balcony. Take short siestas. Visit a park. Call your friends. Read a chapter of a book. All these things easily fit into your day, and not only they help you relax, they also help you focus more and make you more efficient, thus saving more of your time in the future."

I looked at her. Maybe she had a point. After all, she always looked fresh, while a constant cloud of tiredness was around me. To think of it, it was ages ago that I actually did any of the things she said. I had lost contacts and friends. I had stopped reading. I didn't know any new songs. I had let these things go, and however difficult it was to say it aloud, I did miss them. To run away from these missings, I started immersing myself more and more into my work. I thought if I kept myself and my brain busy, I'd never pine for these things again. And it worked.

Until now.

"I get you," I said. "I'll start trying to add these things into my day."

"Back," she said.

"What?" I asked, baffled.

"You need to add these things back into your life. Reintroduce them."

I smiled. I wasn't completely gone, I guess.

"Oh look, the Big Bear," she pointed to the sky.

I looked up, and the sky was refreshingly clear that day. The Big Bear shone down on us, and on seeing the dark sky, the lateness of the hour dawned upon me.

"Mommy," I asked her mockingly, "can we go home now?"

She laughed and punched me on my shoulder. We began walking home, arm in arm with she cosying up to me under the streetlights.

"That reminds me," I asked, "How far along are you on the semester thesis?"

She groaned.

It's really worth to have someone your polar opposite constantly around you, reminding you of what you're not. That way, you complete each other. And as Chili Davis said, 'growing old is compulsory, growing up is optional.'

So maybe I need to make her grow up a little.

And maybe she needs to reawaken the child in me.

"The child is in me still and sometimes not so still."

— Fred Rogers, The World According to Mister Rogers: Important Things to Remember

The Walls That Are Supposed To Be

I was supposed to be asleep.

Then again, I was supposed to have done a lot of things by now in my life.

It is really a pain, this word; 'supposed'. It brings about weights of expectations unmet, fear of challenges ahead and total mayhem in the present.

Who decides what anyone is supposed to do?
Hierarchy, I hear, and I deflate a little.

Who decides what anyone is supposed to be?
Society, I hear, and I deflate a little more.

Who decides what anyone is supposed to say, think or behave like?
Culture, you say and I lose some more.

And finally, why do they decide that I am what I am supposed to be made into?
Because they are supposed to?

Sigh.

But I refused to be one of those who melt easily and are moulded into what they are told they are supposed to be. I refused to be another one devoured by the whims of others and buried due to a lack of fight. Hence, I decided to challenge the norm, and be what I think what I am supposed to be.

Then again, how did I decide what I was supposed to be? If I do not give power to people and things around me, how can I be sure I alone am worthy of that same power? If I don't allow anyone with their flaws to decide for me; how can I, with all my faults, be the judge? If nobody controls me, how am I to be sure I can control myself?

However, the fact remains that this is the one life I have been given, just the one. If I do not retain the rights to make my choices for myself, particularly after being an adult, then it refutes the very point of living this one precious life. So, in a very conceited way - my life, my decisions.

So, where have my decisions taken me?

To places hitherto unknown?
Yes.

To routes which unleashed my creativity?
Yes.

To the avenues of wanted growth in the same creativity?
Not really.

To lengths, I wanted to reach?
Not really.

To the life I wanted?
I don't think so.

To the love I desired?
Definitely not.

Then how am I different? I refused to enter a sphere and decided to build one of my own. I decided to put myself nowhere at first, then chose to prioritise myself; and neither choices have been kind to me. I realise, then, that there is a lot more important than a mere individual. Be it me, or anyone else.

I used to give others preference over me.
I burnt my hands.

Then I stood back and gave myself the baton.
I froze myself out.

I realised that there are a lot more things going about. People are different. What others are supposed to be isn't what I am supposed to be. I wasn't the only one who's acted against the supposing. And I wasn't the only one to have been allowed to do so, as humbling as it may seem. Everyone has their own different scenarios, events, choices and whims. And I needed to handle those differences. And by that, it meant handling myself better.

There are a hundred walls between me and what *I* think I'm supposed to be. Eighty of which depend on my choices and twenty which depend on something that is never controllable, envisioned, and noted for. Fate. Fate, the absolutely nonsensical idea of giving it up, putting your hands up in the air and hoping for whatever storm that is going to hit you. Fate - the excuse us puny humans give when we have no idea what we have to do. The excuse we have when we have no visualisation of whatever we've done was correct or not. The hope we contain that whatever happens, happens for the best.

So, is it all fate? Is my struggle to swim against the tide futile? Am I only a faux revolutionary, and that too only in my mind? Are all the micro changes that I made, the fight, the difficulties, all useless? Do all the roads lead to that one destination; that one predefined end, determined by none other than, the pesky fate?

I certainly do not believe so.

So what if all my decisions point to an end similar to what was supposed to be, supposed by others? If I can even drag that end a couple of degrees today, it will end up quite far off from what it was supposed to be.

That's what it is. A small change today. A little effort today. Some breaking of shackles; today. For a brighter tomorrow, just how you supposed it to be. As they say, there's no need to change boats, change the direction and your shores change akin.

I owned every second that this world could give,
I saw so many places,
The things that I did,
Yeah, with every broken bone,
I swear I lived!

– I Lived, OneRepublic

THE PHOENIX'S PYRE

Fire blazed all around, embers and the heat threatening the soles of my feet. Above me I saw layers of crimson, red and maroon; intermingling with painful shades of yellow and orange. Cracks appeared where I was, and lava seeped through. I stood on an island of coal which was rapidly succumbing to the conflagration, greatly diminishing from all sides. Soon I will only have a circle to stand on, which will be the last of my solid footing. Scorching winds threatened to melt off my face, and the hair on my body had already been singed to the skin. Burns were slowly erupting all over the body, as I proficiently managed to breathe from the ashes and coal dust. Inferno it was; full of anguish, pain, and roasting.

It is difficult for me to often accept and apportion my affectionate nihilism and my willingness to sit back with a drink and watch the world burn. Which is as acceptable to many as it is comfortable for me. Nevertheless, there are a few who'd help me mix the drinks. People who have chosen the third side in a dichotomy and the fourth in a trichotomy. People who violently debate with themselves within, but remain unruffled on the surface, with a grin that's often interpreted as a smirk. People who question every notion of power and authority internally, yet with a nod to the omnipresent evident hypocrisy grab it with both hands. People who know their flaws, but neither do they wear it as armour nor do they let them weaken them - they acknowledge them as what they are, traits which shape them equally as the strengths. People, who do not plan world domination, but neither do they allow any encroachment in their own spheres.

People tend to stay away from us. Not because of what we look like, we look pretty normal, thank you very much. It's for how we look at life like. It's easier to accept a strangled sense of abandonment when it is due to your inner outcast, rather than your outer anomaly. For what it's worth, we dislike having most people around us too, so that suits us. We've spiralled into the sea of perceived madness, but we weren't pushed. We fell on our backs into it, arms outstretched, with closed eyes and a mirthless smile on our face. The question then, is what drove us to the edge.

What drove us? Neither wrongs nor rights. Never good nor bad. We walked past the average choices. We tore open the gates of tendentious righteousness barred via a thick smog of hollow and pretentious morality; guarded by the fragile arms of society's respect and norms. The most important player, however, came from us ourselves. We thought. We were skeptics - are too, if not more. We thought more than the average brain, and modesty was never our virtue. If you think, you eventually question things and their value to the extent of total futility. Futility of purpose, need, and legitimate-ness. We sought a black cat in a dark room, a cat which was definitely there, until we reached the abyss and it stopped; glared at us and leaped.

Much to Nietzche's vindication, we looked into the abyss and it returned the favour. We weren't the only ones there - many were retrieved by 'counselors'; and many shivered at the abyss.

" ..We both looked into the abyss, but when it looked back at us, you blinked."

– Batman, Justice League: Crisis on Two Earths

Humanity needs cages, mankind needs borders. A sense of belonging isn't the cause of the border, it is the root of it. But inside the borders, there are voices - voices which whisper and scream, reason and argue about the matters within and out. These voices are in us all, you and me included. They are in the multitude, some louder than the others, while the others are more convincing. We didn't choose the loudest or the most convincing, as most do, we listened to them all. We gave each voice a platform to stand on it's own, giving it the required opportunity to justify and make sense. We refused to be the judge, bound by a set of established laws, and instead became the jury - with our own reasoning and logic to feed upon. Which is why we ended up on the edge, we weren't there as an accident. We were there because we chose to be there.

Maybe we are more enticed towards Lucifer's Inferno than Christ's Heaven. Closer, on the periphery, we've seen the brochures of both. We refuse the gates of heaven and stay adrift of the volcano of hell. And from above the hell and beneath the heaven, we see the beauty of hell and the darker undertones of heaven, and we smile.

Never belonged then, nor now.

I looked below as lava approached my feet, and I heard a cry. It was more of a screech, coming from something fearless. It wasn't a cry of fear, it was as natural as a wolf's howl at full moon. It was the cry of a beast in his habit, habitat and comfort. As I looked up, a majestic bird came into view, with colours of scarlet and gold, a plumage of fire, and a tail of shining amber. It shrieked at me, as I raised my hands. It lifted me up, and carried me away as the last of my old footing succumbed to the inferno. I saw a sea of fire, and as the bird rose up and up, I could see the beauty of an ablaze bottom.

I knew that far far above me were the cool winds of heaven, where sweet music played of the lyre, but I knew I belonged only in the phoenix's pyre.

Yours Truly; You.

Dear Future Me;

I hope, first of all, that this letter finds you. Secondly, I hope it finds you well.

There are many theories of how a future self can help a younger self, but knowing me so far I can tell you that you, from the future, wouldn't change a thing or give me any word of advice. That's because you're still me, and I firmly wouldn't go back to any of my even younger selves. I wouldn't change a thing - no righting a wrong, no advice to aid in protection, and no reliving old good happiness - as I deeply understand that I am what I am because of what I've seen, done and learnt. And since I - and we - are thus so self aware that we know what we have been through is what shaped us, you wouldn't send me a letter even if you could.

So then, now comes the part where I talk to you about why I'd like to tell you some things.

I cannot hope to be a teacher to you here, as by simple mathematics you have more years in you, which includes more experiences and lessons than I in my current state can finitely hold. I do, however, distinctly hope that within these words I can be a reminder to you about the things I remember now but are maybe forgotten as I approach your age. These things are small things, but that doesn't mean they aren't significant enough.

Picking up on that note, I want you to remind you of the lesson you learnt while on a walk back home one fine evening when you were struck by the idea of a letter you could write. The idea struck you, but for months at long you couldn't work out a way to formulate it into reality, so you let it be. The subconscious (a thing which fails me today, hope you have it figured out better) however, didn't let it go, and sat on it for a good two years until one fine night it hatched into a piece of detailed inspiration; and you sat down to write it then; which eventually turned out into what you're reading now.

You must remind yourself constantly that ideas need refining, and they mature and evolve at their own rate at times.

You must also recall the realisation you had that night; that even if you had the refined idea on the footpath during the walk, you wouldn't have been able to pen it down the way you did two years later. You accepted the fact that back then you had just begun writing, and the idea you had required much more sophisticated skills than the ones in your arsenal. Within the next two years our growth of skill was precocious - as defined by the use of precocious - and thus you managed to jot the idea down to the justice it deserved. Maybe you, as a reader now can say that you can do a better job, and thus by making you realise that I have done my job today.

You must remind yourself that skills improve with practice and time, and some projects and achievements require different levels of the same skill set.

Throughout my life so far, I have been a terrible starter. Part of me hopes you've rectified that in the span between my today and your today. Part of me thinks it's something that we just are, a klutz who just starts slow. If in case it is the latter, I want to remind you of how you always manage to grow into the role eventually, and douse the fires of people questioning you. People questioned us before and after our +2, and while it took a different amount of time for both cases of growth, we eventually ended up getting respect, admiration, and most importantly, credit. We learnt from where we were, and picked ourselves up to raise our heads high.

You must remind yourself that a slow start can always be the backbone of progress, that a man's development may be gradual or rapid; but it should be positive and upwards.

Decision making is a part and parcel of life, and you know that as much as I do, probably even more. So if you're facing pain due to a wrong decision or fearing pain due to it, I want to remind you of all the wrong decisions you've made. I want you to recall all the setbacks you think they've given, including the regrets, losses and, pain. Think about how they were insurmountable then, impossible to escape from. Think about how you had almost forgotten them before I asked you to reminisce about them. And I want you to then see where you are right now.

You must remind your heart that life keeps on going; anyhow, anyway, anytime, anywhere.

You must remember our first love. Not because of the cliched notions of first love but because I am so much of myself because of it, I am sure you're much more thanks to it. Turns out, our first love was our greatest teacher which inflicted a great punishment - but that punishment reaped lessons. I want you to remember the sweetness of it, the pleasant nothingness of it. I want you to recall the passionate, irresponsible, and irrelevant happiness it caused. After that, I want you to remember succinctly why you let go the idea of love. Both, you and I know we did love after that, but we focused on being something worthwhile. We realised that a knight in a shining armour has neither his mettle nor metal tested. Yet, we needed love and it got to us from people we never thought would, and from places we never even thought twice about. Recall and reassure that belief in you that love has its way.

Keep reminding yourself that love will find you when you most need it, and it will heal you where you most need it.

It has always been our story – to seek redemption or esteem via the batons of acceptance and tolerance. So far, I seem to have failed to grasp those batons properly. Acceptance has led to a spike in my ignorance, and since I do not like ignorance, I opt for tolerance. And tolerance tests my patience. While I am currently swinging between the two, it is an imperative need for me to find a middle ground, which I hope you've achieved. If not, you continue to struggle to this day. I want you to remember the struggles in all accumulation, as someday it will bear the fruit of a result.

You must keep on reminding yourself that neither you nor I am the finished product, that we still share some flaws and needs some things to iron out.

So, there you go. I hope you've enjoyed a this little flashback as much as I look forward to becoming you. Of course, there in the future you may disagree with what I seem to have staunchly vested on, and if that's the case, I'd love to stumble upon the idea and see if I can refurbish what I have here.

Before I take your leave, I hope I put a smile on your face.

I remain me,

Yours truly;

You.

Rein The Rain

The hilly air gushed around. The mild sun played with a careless peepal beside me and wove pretty netted patterns onto the stone floor. Beyond the broken wall of the once regal fort, a sea of green littered with inglorious specks of human civilization, which extended until my brain changed its focus onto the darkening sky. The wind became chilly as I looked up and closed my eyes. Lengthy seconds passed by as a pure droplet splattered on my cheek.

Within a jiffy the entire land was wet. The trees rejoiced a well deserved cleanse, the soil spread it's divine petrichor and people began scrambling around me as I stood there, hands on the old brick railing, getting soaked.

The water flowing off me seemed to take away a lot with it. Dark things, which are not easily described yet are so abundant. With each passing second, as my clothes began to get heavier, my soul began to feel lighter. My lips curled into a smile, and gradually widened into a laugh - the truest, purest laugh I'd laughed in quite a while.

It is weird how continuity is taken as a measure to avoid drastic changes, yet the most subtle and influential changes happen within great spans of continuity. Between days and weeks of a stifling monotone, change sets in disguised and veiled, slowly pushing out things that were once indisputable. As time passes by, everything seems to remain the same, and suddenly one day you reflect and compare and see that you are losing hair, friends, love, and life, not necessarily in any order. Once the realization hits you, acceptance follows in it's own sweet time.

It's like finally getting used to the scorching Indian summer, until a drop from the sky splashes onto you and you realise, that everything will be the same, but not really the same.

But I do not want to think about how the monsoon heralds a new change for me. I do not want to think about how difficult it has been so far. I just want to stand there, get drenched, and laugh. I do not want to care that the people around me may think of me as a lunatic. I've been through a scorching summer – the longest one so far in my life, and it has left behind burns. The rainwater soothes those burns.

I was used to the summer of my life – burning, scalding, and unrewarding. Toiling under the sun is supposed to be a chore for the strongest, which is, frankly, a blithering lie. It is such a hopeless environment; it ends your will, beats your motivation, and destroys your belief. What sustains you is either a lunatic determination to live, or a dogged discipline to endure. Moreover, the ordeal is lonely. It is not lonely as in 'no one to talk to'. It is lonely as in the dearth of your own sane voice conversing with you. I repeat, this toil is not for the strongest, for strength is the disguised and veiled change that sets in within this infernial monotone. If you see it through, you see the rains.

But I have a problem with rains. If there's summer, I can tell that the days will be hot, every day. But if there's monsoon, it may rain thrice in a day or never in three days. And if it rains for three days straight... let's say even someone like me who can manage huge droughts is afraid of a flood.

But the first rain is different. It symbolizes a transition, a frustrating period of time when it doesn't rain enough to drive out the heat truly, and afterwards the sauna like warmth is twice as problematic – simply because no one is prepared for it.

That, is a kind of transition I am in. I was prepared for everything in the past with a few trusted tools in my arsenal, ones which may not be good enough for what I need next.

Case in point - music. I have my own playlist; tailored and stitched to my need. It had every type of music I needed; for the times I was on the road, in my bed, when I was up, or when I was down. But now? That very playlist bores me. Songs which I used to listen on repeat are changed as soon as I hear the first beats. Similarly, things I was extremely excited to read and enjoyed reading no longer catch my fancy. Things that sustained and greased my monotone are now stumbling blocks which halted my progress into the transition.

This problem is very much alike my life conundrum - similar to something I've solved before while not truly the same. As much as disguised a change may be, it has the potential to provide me with my counter to it. As much as internal the pain may be, it itself has the requirements to be my medicine. Maybe I need to change my songs which cater to the new rains in my life. Maybe I need different books which talk about the rains.

The first rain, true to its fickle self, stopped abruptly. I ran my hand through my hair, slicked them back, and gazed around. The dust had settled, and at least for the time being, the environment was cool. Slowly the warmth grew along with the wind - but it only made me feel cooler; thanks to being wet to the bone. The smile on my face stayed on.

Epiphanies are to life what a surprise, non seasonal rain is to a hot day, they give you a new perspective, a fresh outlook and a sense of relief. But more than that, they provide you with an hitherto unnoticed way of dealing with things - however unorthodox or unconventional it may seem.

That day I learnt that to avoid the sauna-like uncomfortable warmth after the first rains during the seasonal transition period, get soaked in the said rain. Who cares what others have to say? It is *my* rain. I deserve it.

The transition will be littered with plentiful rains, and as this first rain gave me a great epiphany, I'm sure other showers will defninitely provide more.

I need to search for my rains, keep them, and enjoy them.

If I get a cold, well, that's another disguised change, and I'm sure I'll find a way through it too.

Feel it, tame it,
love the pain.
Breathe it, smell it,
rein the rain.

O Death, Do Us Part

A scythe is clutched in her bony hand. Her face is hidden in darkness beneath a hood. Her pitch black endless robe is flowing behind her. The Grim Reaper stands in front of me, her other arm extended towards me. Her blood red eyes almost seem kind, full of pity and remorse, probably even guilt. Her form radiates power, yet she seems fragile, as if the millions of souls she's reaped have cursed her. Her extended arm may not be to escort my soul to purgatory. It may just be an extension of friendship, from a loner surrounded by the dead to another, surrounded by the living.

Put a scythe on my throat and I won't flinch. I wouldn't worry about dying, nor would I be afraid of the suffering. The prospect of death doesn't intimidate me - if I die, I die. Yet, there's a newfound indifference in me about death, for now I don't even seem to care about who will be affected if and when I die. Death, if it ever arrives, I pray it arrives stealthily and takes me silently. I hope to be taken in isolation - invisible, unnoticed and unrealised - very much like the way I've lived.

Earlier, I did not know who will cry when I die. Now, I don't care about it. People may wish to be remembered after their death as good people, and usually, death grants them that wish. I've seen people turn up to funerals of the wicked, for cowards hate to be painted with the brush of sentimental judgement which crumbles logic. I, on the other hand, wish to die; and wish to die alone. Let me be ravaged by the vultures and the scavengers, for that's how humanity's vultures have always picked on me. Let me be eaten by the dirt, making me dust, therefore allowing me to belong somewhere truly. Let there not be a funeral, for I do not want pretentiously pious people praying for me when all they did was prey on me. Let there not be gatherings of people with remorse or regret, for I hold no grudge. Let there not be any tears of acid which will corrode me even after I am gone. I wasn't truly there with you, and please, when I really go, let me go in peace, even if I am in pieces.

Yet, life purges in me and prevents me from grasping her hand. Our need for each other is forbidden, for as uncanny it is for a mortal to voluntarily seek death as a friend, it is totally unheard of death seeking a suitor.

She 'lives' for me, and I 'die' for her everyday. There's something about love which baffles everyone. And there's something about death that mystifies everyone. It is forbidden to mix love and death, but often the unloved seek love in death; and the loved fear the lack of love in it. Forbidden it may be, but to live and belove death is my choice, and to be death and belove a life is hers. Something has to go. Either she gives in, or I give up.

It's as if there's a wall… and my life is in it, trapping me away from her. Life that is enclosed within walls which cannot be broken, but can be jumped over or dug out of. Walls of pious prayers, of societal norms, of staple love and conditioned minds. Essentially, it is life that remains the same regardless of what happens beyond the walls. But she's there, beyond the walls, alone, and waiting. I cannot see her, but I can feel her need. Unless of course, I manage to break the boundaries and jump over the walls..

I don't know if I can. And the walls are closing in.

"Kaaga Re Kaaga Re Mori Itni Araj Tose;
Chun Chun Khaiyo Maans!
Arajiya Re Khaaiyo Na Tu Naina More,
Khaaiyon Na Tu Naina;
Mohe Piya Ke Milan Ki Aas!"

TRANSLATION: O Crow, I have only this request to you,
eat every bit of (my body's) flesh,
but do not eat my eyes,
don't eat my eyes
as I have a wish to see my lover..

बिस्तर TO BISTRO

My tongue is busy, moving around and sloshing it. I feel around its periphery; prodding, poking and wetting it. I licked at it, tried to lift certain parts. Almost as if it could feel my efforts, juices secreted from it's within, bringing with it a familiar taste. Slowly some other stuff came off, giving a feeling of pleasure that was oh so satisfying. Encouraged, I doubled my efforts. But after a few minutes, it was still the same. No progress and even the wetness was gone. I gave up.

Having a fenugreek (*saunf*) seed stuck perfectly between your skewed wisdom teeth is a huge pain.

As I walk out after my meal, I focus on what change the past six months have given. When you move from a small town to a big city, things are supposed to change. And things did change. I was thrust into a completely new way of life, and when I decided to nest in the historically profound and thus, the posh area of the city, I met with - not a culture shock - but a 'ah this is it' kinda shock.

I am not a hillbilly. Though of course certain sections of people from my current nest may call me that. I prefer the term '*desi,*' or even a coded sitcom reference. I am, quite clearly, the '*Indravardhan Sarabhai*' to my (and many people's) '*Maya Sarabhai.*' I have talked with certain friends who are a little 'Maya,' and it was so far fun to point out certain nonplussing differences.

Case on point, a girl said, "**Today mom is cooking *methi*** ke parathe**!**"

"Girl, we are Gujjus, and they are called *Theplas*."

However, nothing beats a typical English loving high profile girl trying to flaunt her vocab: "Can I have a USB battery?"

"What?"

"A USB battery!"

"You mean a power bank?"

It is not like I haven't been to cities ever. I have been to and lived in cities - tier II at best. But they were easy places and I wasn't out of place. When I told people that I am shifting to these cities, no one felt the need to warn me, or give me tips stemming from their experiences from said cities. However, when I did announce my move to the Big City™, there were floods of people telling me to handle myself well, not get carried away, and don't lose focus. I was warned, threatened even, to not attain any snob, and if I do, I must not bring it back home. I think it was more about not losing the touch to my roots.

And I have gladly stayed true to those, I think.

The differences were minute but great. The commute suddenly became a very public, and often compromising affair from being a leisurely private affair. And worse, complaining about it would make you sound like a wuss. People would travel for 300 minutes daily and still call themselves from the same city. I can change states via train, take a rickshaw, go to my real home and take a bath and that person could still be travelling in the same 'city'. Or, I could take a flight to Dubai and they'd still be chugging in the public transport. And dare you insinuate that they are not locals.

Time flies. The city never stops. The sleep is just a necessity to get going the next day. I was used to the proper comfort of my own bed (बिस्तर) – cozy, confortable and **mine.** Here it is just a pitstop to return to and go again.

Food – while I love good food, getting the equivalent of good taste in big cities often means long travel or high costs, sometimes both. Until I rediscovered taste in small restaurants. The only comfort at the end of a day was often the food at a familiar bistro.

Lot more changes. New people. New life. New factors and a special *maidan*. Yet, somehow it still has accepted me but tells me not to get too comfortable. Very much like a stuck fenugreek seek in your wisdom tooth.

Like a new girlfriend who keeps you on your toes, this new city is keeping me on my heels.

Between "The city of dreams" and "The city that never sleeps;" I am trapped into a sleepless dream. I don't know when I'll sleep or when the dream will end.

But from बिस्तर to Bistro, I will always be grateful to my journey.

To Lull in a Null

The pendulum clock chimes five, as I throw away my beddings in frustration. Once again, the night had left me petrified of slumber.

My sleeplessness worries me this time, for it is not due to the usual causes. Quite often the woke hours of the night are due to an extreme in my emotional spectrum - but not today. Today I was stable, balanced, and totally in control. Except for the control of my sleep.

I have always craved balance. In all my endeavours, beliefs, and workings; 'balance' is the crucial hinge around which my life moves. It is this tendency to stay in the centre, to stand in the middle has left me often neither here nor there. I did not belong on the left, nor did I accept the right. Up north was too weird, down south was too uncomfortable.

For years I thought that if I did not belong anywhere, it was because there was something wrong with me. Why wouldn't I see things so obvious to many others? Why were things so clear to me invisible to others? Was it due to some sort of deformity in my brain? Or was I in a very unique closet which shrouded my vision and outlook? Was I too protected to see things as they really are? Am I a convoluted version of Gautama before he became the Buddha?

Preposterous it was - the notion of comparing myself to a mythical god. But something needed to be done - cracks needed to be filled and creases needed to be ironed. The fabric of my being was required to be flawless.

Then the reason for my tense, open eyes hit me. I realised that the sleeplessness is an act of rebellion of my subconscious, not like a soldier standing up to a tyrant but a teenaged kid standing up to his busy father for not being attentive enough. My feed to my subconscious was often like the questions I posed a while ago, and very recently they had been replaced, curtly enough, by enquiries pertaining to the viability, longevity and legitimation of a journey I had picked in the last six months. The focus invariably shifted from 'I, me myself' to 'us', and my subconscious felt ignored and betrayed, for it was always the answer provider, and now it often had no answers. It complained of having its stature demoted and value depreciated. It complained to me, about me finding other schools of thought as compared to mine only.

Do you know how difficult it is to manage a subconscious which is having an identity crisis? It isn't like parenting a particularly rebellious teenager, it is like trying to 'parent' your once unquestioned matriarch of the family who now needs help with the same things your child needs but thinks they are too old for that. They were once the doers and the decision makers, who cannot take the reality that time now, once again, asks them questions they do not know the answer to, and trust me, they really do not like not knowing. More so they do not like conceding their lack of knowledge, not because of haught, but because of the still residual need to be seen in control, in power.

My subconscious then is a 90-year-old grandma in the body of an 18-year-old boy. It is a terrifying combination, not only fancy to fixated minds which cannot be moved but also sporting young energy to battle it out with you, word by word. 'Old brain on young shoulders' gone very wrong. Naturally then, without any fault of it, it becomes a warehouse of negative notions and vicious paranoia, which stays in until it overflows and ruins a night or two.

You think you are prepared for a gap in your monotone and it goes well for a couple of days until that honeymoon period ends. Then the time of the day that was 'theirs' starts looking at you expectantly, and since you have no company, you turn back to the very same grumpy subconscious who was waiting for this chance to create havoc in your mind.

I was wrong, the sleeplessness *was* due to an emotional high, but today it wasn't in the aftermath of it, but it was the warning of it. Like the din before a storm and few seconds of eye-to-eye contact before two warriors start their battle to the death, this was a call to locate sleep and escape if I could. Because my subconscious was about to start it's fear-mongering, self-hatred and sensory overloads - and this time, it had the ammunition since months, and had raised interest on its intentions.

Fear caught me. Fear of loss, of abandonment, of not being fought for and of having to bear it all alone. But hey, haven't I been here before? I've dealt with these fears before, and that's when I realised that we do not fear a new fear, we're always scared of an experience happening again. I wasn't particularly afraid of walking the road alone, I have done it voluntarily many times. I was afraid of being thrown alone on the road, to travel to the ends alone, broken and weak, *again*.

I twist and turn on my bed as the paranoia grips me.

Self-loathe returns, mocking me about my dependency, once more. But this time, it was more vicious, as it knew the dependency was different. It isn't a dependency of 'can not do anything worthwhile without them', it is a dependency that affects the core of a human. It is the dependency that hits you when you try to sleep after your normal day and you realise that the option to depend on them is suspended. It is the dependency to share the smallest things and to wish them beside you when the monotone wavers, but realising that the option isn't there. This dependency is the cruellest arrow in the quiver of Cupid, and it pains when you really don't need anything more to feel.

I sit up and hold my head into my hands.

Suddenly everything annoys me. That one ray of streetlight from the window which would beautify the room every night, now hurt my eyes. The small clicking noise from the fan made me want to throw a pillow at it, the same pillow which was so annoyingly refusing to be in proper shape the whole night. The water I try to gulp is too warm. The t-shirt I am wearing is too hot. Everything is hopeless here.

"ENOUGH," I say to myself, as I get up. I pace about the room in agony as I notice my work bag, and I realise that my ultimate holy water to the demon of my subconscious was already with me.

I remove her stole from the bag, the stole I stole right before our last meet, and I felt I had I just gotten hold of the golden fleece.

I went to bed, draped the stole around my face and breathed, engulfing myself in her scent. Afraid to drive that scent out of the smooth cloth, I exhaled away from it. And there and then, my sensory overload died, the self-hate was conquered by my love for her, and the fear gave way to assurance. I was calm. Sleep smiled at me now.

She was there.

What do you say to your bratty, senile subconscious?

Not today.

My Epiphany is a B

I have a very queer relationship with my epiphanies. They've been my door to revelations and discoveries, the gateway to realisations and uncomfortable shower moments. They have, in fact built to be the conscious self I am and have shaped the conscience I have.

As I have a pathological need to anthropomorphise everything I love and everything I deem important; this, thus is an attempt to imagine what if my epiphanies were collectively an invisible friend, very much human, and very much communicative. The idea is a quintessential 4 am one, and since I am prone to (and happily guilty of) writing at the dawn of the day, I pick up the pen (by that I mean, open the laptop).

My Epiphany™ then, portrayed itself to my annoyingly active and wildly superfluous imagination as a splendid woman I'm in a weird relationship with - she was ravishing to look at and ravaging to deal with. Like a strong business woman who'd be your boss, telling you she's your friend but doing the bare minimum to be called one. Sure, she'd help you out sometimes, but since you sadly understand the law of averages you figure out her talk was going to fit in place somewhere.

She'd be around sometimes, being the *Betaal to my Vikram,* filling my ears in regarding everything that I do - a live commentary in my ears which I definitely DID NOT need.

"Oh hey, you could have walked that route dude, sorry I didn't remind you you've been here before."

Ugh.

"Oooh, that girl saw you pick your nose yesterday, don't expect her to say hello to you."

Sigh.

"And, when your boss said to check the view from the office balcony he actually meant to know you better and you told him you have pending work, hahahahaha doofus."

Gee, thanks.

"And also, you've left the house keys on the door today."

What!?

"Yeah, pretty stupid of you. Also, you must finish three projects today or your appraisal is gone, you've already told your boss you're lagging, idiot."

Damn you.

Sometimes, she isn't anywhere nearby you. For a while it's brilliant. Life is awesome, you live without fear, without nagging, and without consideration. You live a life that is happy, joyous, bountiful. You see no wrong, you do no wrong and you care about no wrong.

Until one fine day, you're grinning and working on your desk, and she pops in, with binders and dossiers of notes and cumulative talks of what blunders and nonsense you've perpetrated thus far.

"Three weeks ago. The salesman actually, very elaborately scammed you of three thousand bucks."

WHAT!?

"Last week, your landlord's young daughter heard you listening to some explicit songs, and has been singing it aloud in front of him, hence those texts."

Goddamn it.

"That office girl still thinks you're disgusting, she saw you sneeze into your hands and wipe them on your trousers yesterday."

Great.

"And also," she said with a definitive smirk, "the stunning girl at the cafe yesterday was actually hitting on you."

REALLY? I WAIT.. yeah she was. ARGH.

It was an abusive relationship.

Enough, I decided. I need to stand up and get things going in my favour. Next time she pops in with her snark I'm not taking her nonsense.

So it happened. One fine day I was working in the office when I had to get some forms filled by my boss – some kind of performance review. I went in, explained the necessary and he smiled, "Okay fill in the form and bring it to me."

Confused, I told him, "Sir, you have to review me in this form."

Sir replied, almost absentmindedly, "I'll sign it. Fill it."

I left the cabin, back to my seat, confused.

Epiphany™ couldn't resist. She yelled in my ear, "HE'S GIVING YOU THE OPPORTUNITY TO RATE YOURSELF YOU DUMBO"

I got that. Processed it. But I did want to retaliate.

"YEAH WHY COULDN'T YOU TELL ME THIS IN THE OFFICE, SMARTY?"

She looked stunned. I, the silent listener, actually fired back at her. I actually had confronted her. She tried to speak but no word came out. She slowly turned and walked away.

The voiceless had found a voice. Loud and clear. It was like the first time an adolescent retorts back at a parent. Like the slaves of Yunkai fighting back. Sirius Black's escape from Azkaban. For her, it was probably the revolt of 1857. The French Revolution. Vive La Superego.

I went back home chuffed with myself. Changed, ate and went to bed.

Just as I was about to turn the light off, I saw her at the base of my bed.

She looked different.

Her hair was now short, bob-cut with purple streaks. Her eyes had strong, black makeup. She wore a loose black, death metal T-shirt. Khakhi, baggy trousers. Tattoos on her arm. Piercings on her nose and face. A complete deadpan and resting bitch face.

Without wasting a second she spoke, loudly, without emotion, in an unwavering tone.

"People have always alienated you because you remind them of what they aren't. You give love but don't get it back, from anywhere. Not even from yourself."

My eyes went wide with horror. My soul wept. My superego whimpered and apologized. My heart slowed down.

Oh, my word. Oh, my-my.

WHAT HAVE I DONE!?

The Other Arrow of Eros

I sit, engrossed in my work, staring at the laptop screen. Time seemed to dawdle past me, while in reality, it was gushing past me quicker than I realised. I sat back, and sipped from my cup of hot coffee, when suddenly my senses awakened and I felt a rush of cold air through my hair.

I looked up, and saw that it was raining. The cool breeze that accompanies rains had turned into gusts, and I saw trees swaying violently, people rushing for cover and safety outside the door of the cafe. I got up and walked to the large French window.

Coffee in one hand, the other a part of my folded arms, I stare at the window. The droplets of fresh rain seemed to race against each other, clearing the mist on the panels simultaneously. Vague shades of lights and other colours came through my eyes as blurs, muted patters of the raindrops bouncing on the roof shed outside seemed to cater to a peculiar melancholy. I hold the cup with both hands and sip once, and take in a deep breath.

Work was always going to be a drug to drive you out of zone you don't want to be, but what happenes if that very zone houses your home? How trepid it would be to go out and fight the world, and eventually come back to your own shelter and lose? Is it even a loss, one that counts, if you know you have to fight the same battle again, the next night? Is this perpetual battle to win - win against the world and my world - the definition of my life?

Funnily, this battle is one of the things many will not understand, at least, that is what I hope. I do not like to think many people live in such trepidation of their own skin and mind, and if they do, it shows a real dark undertone to colours of life.

This battle has been set onto me after liberation. Yes, liberation. I was liberated, from the shackles I placed on myself, and entered an arena where I battle the beast of my creation, and his blessing.

I sit on the couch, clench my knees around my clasped hands and layman head on the backrest and stare at the light right on my face. Any time now, the beast will arrive, and we will spar again. The beast, of course, is none other than independence, and within that independence is a certain dependence anchored within me. The beast is armed with the bow of Eros, with all but one arrow in his quiver, one which hits me every day, one whose counterpart hits a certain someone everyday as well, I think. The beast has an essence of my belief in myself, the poise of my own confidence, and the glow of my own strength.

My beast is none other than my own lineament.

Paradoxical, isn't it? How can my own characteristics, distinguishing and positive ones at that, be the source of my own troubles, stemming from my own cognition? You'd think people would target my weaknesses to break me. Little do they know I break myself every day when the sun sets, and gather my pieces every morning.

Thats the thing, the world attacks your weaknesses, and in turn, may end up building you up. I attack my own strengths, and in turn, end up disregarding them and breaking myself.

But no. Recently I realised that I am not attacking my strengths. I am attacking, and probably searching for the source of my strengths. I am searching for that anchor of dependency which has been holding my independence steady. I am searching for the other arrow of Eros.

There are some strengths that I had, and I had build a stone pillar around them. Some strengths I had stuck in the freezer, some strengths I had packed and thrown in the dingiest corners of the attic of my personality. And try as hard as I could, I failed to break the walls or thaw the ice, or find the strengths within me again.

Until he showed up.

He healed me from wounds I never showed, nor did I ever mention. He ironed the creases of doubt within my own esteems, built a hard hitting system of belief in me. He took out the frozen courage and thawed it, slowly and excruciatingly. He chiselled on the pillar housing my fight, and made me rediscover the warrior within me. He found the packet of conviction I couldn't locate to save my life, and gifted it back to me.

He made me, me again. And in that process, I lost some bits of myself too, to him, and finally came to be me again.

And very much like how a crushed magnet still searches for its bits and pieces, I am still looking for the bits I lost to him.

Every night, I do not attack my own strengths, I search them for him.

I realise that my independence is one of the greatest gifts I have. I understand that my lineament is the biggest legacies of him.

I don't attack my lineament. I scourge the legacy, and I search for him.

I search for the other arrow of Eros.

Abiit Nemine Salutato

There exists a quiet void within everything. And when I say everything, I mean every thing, ranging from the commotion of the day to the inherent inactivity of the night. This void is one that fills, and it fills in more than what you can imagine - it is located within the biggest of minds and the tiniest of matter. Even atoms, the stuff that quite literally is what we and everything around us is made of, are empty.

Such omnipresence. It is a shame then, that mankind has focused on what one is full of, conveniently ignoring the fact that people are emptier than you think. Maybe it is the lack of knowledge, a completely another type of emptiness, which leads to that search. Or it is the willful ignorance of knowledge; and the willingness to stay ignorant that probably reeks out as emptiness within this ostensible life.

And I find myself engulfed by this void, and quite often it is the one companion I have throughout my days and nights. When the shadow departs in the night and the ghosts disappear in the day, it is the void that bridges me over each change. It consumes me into it and thus fills me up with what one might say are unwanted thoughts. But that's what you think.

If the thoughts are unwanted, they aren't in the mind. Somehow, in some way, we attract the thoughts we have. They aren't the noise of an overworked machine which is crying for attention. Thoughts are not the ramblings of an old deranged person in an asylum. They are nothing but the observations and inferences that the subconscious carries out without even you knowing. The experiments are vivid, the environment is your life, and the subject is you.

One day you'll be face to face with whatever saw fit to let you exist in this universe, and you'll have to explain the space you've filled. If it is a god, you'll meet him, a god who won't be as merciful as you think he'll be; particularly if you've not abided by his laws. And if it's science, then you'd fit your workings with the help of response and stimulus; causation and correlation; and show that you abided by the laws of science and answer to the void that you had a reason. A reason to do what you did. A reason to be.

So, then, the reasoning in The Court Of The VoidTM has no room for morality. Morality, ethics, being good, is something so abstract that there is essentially no set definition of it, and hence, The Court Of The VoidTM rejects it. What it does respect, are the observations and inferences of experiments, of vivid detail, broad environment, and a specific subject.

So every night, just before I fall asleep, I am summoned into The Court Of The VoidTM and I stand on trial. My offence is to be, and I am accused of being the way I am. I stand in the witness box, and I am interrogated by someone who looks, walks and talks just like me, but I fail to accept him as me. I fight my own case against a rival who, I think is what I should be. And the judge is the empty void, who'd have me declared guilty immediately.

We rally, back and forth, with proof and assumptions; deductions and analysis. Each day my rival comes up with better arguments than before, and each day it becomes more and more difficult to prove him wrong. The case remains unsolved, and the hearing date extends for the subsequent night, every time. Every night, I live to live like me, and fight to be like me.

But it is debilitating. Each night it is tougher than ever to stand up for me, and each night my rival creeps in closer to defeat me. Each night he senses a weakening stance, a meeker argument, and each night he looks for the kill. Every passing night, my sense of me diminishes, and his sense of me thrives a little bit more.

Recently, something different happened. I realised, midway of sparring, that my rival has a case. As the case stretched onto the break of the sun, it dawned upon me that I should not be what I am.

That's when I decided to swap positions. No, not with my rival in The Court Of The Void™ , but with the void itself. I decided to judge myself. And that is because I judge with a ferocity which pierces through the heart of someone in front of me. And when I judge myself, the ferocity often increases, becoming monumental; if not gargantuan.

And I rule. I rule that both parties are wrong. I am not supposed to be what I am, but neither can anyone tell me what to be. I choose to be what I want. If I want to, I can choose to live in the gaps wherein I left the things we never said. I can live in the cracks which I filled with the feelings I discarded. I can live beneath the rocks where I dug the emotions which weren't valued. If I want to, I can live in the lab of my subconscious, and analyse on its experiments. And if I want to, I can very well live within the void which allows me to do all of that, and then let it fill me up with an arsenal of vindication.

I rule that I shall be immortal, by the words that I pen and battles I pick. I shall be immortal for the cowardice I betray and the hesitance I portray. I shall be immortal for the healing I have provided and for the damages I've doled out. I cannot be killed in a way that matters. I shall be immortal because I cannot be killed, for I am one with the void, and the void stays. You know you are in a void. You realise you're in a void. And if you're anything like me, you become the void.

And that was the last hearing.

Case closed.

Abiit Nemine Salutato.

Of Lips and Apocalypse

My talks begin with aplomb, but they never seem to end. Sadly, it is now taken as eloquence.

It is this 'eloquence', which has now provided me with a living. So much so, that my ramblings are taught to students as oratory examples. My moments of going blank are seen as the norm on how to take a pause mid-speech, and my frail voice is portrayed as the elusive skill of voice modulation.

A good man makes money out of his pleasures, a great man makes fortunes from his pain. And greatness is nothing but the absence of hooks on your bowties, the lack of dirt inside your lapels, and the mask of a smile in front of the cameras. Greatness is all and everything of the tautness of your shirt, the narrowness of your trousers and the shine in your boots. Greatness is as perceived as it is experienced, and is as expected as it is probable for me.

I knew roads take you to places, and I knew paths take you to virtue. I had to look down the road and the path, and I had to decide which one to take. I looked down and long along them and saw an end, and so I took out my sharp edge, my sturdy support and began chopping and whatever I saw, trudging along mirthlessly and sadistically, which eventually was documented as stunning and brave. The route I forge ends where I end, and it ends at a tombstone of blood and cries, which might read,

"Apocalypse at his lips."

It is really funny - and it is the only thing I genuinely laugh at now - how my pretentiousness hasn't been unmasked yet. Pretentiousness sells, and it sells at a premium. The world looks at me with a shine in their eyes, and for years I have waited for it to turn into a fire of the heathen. But it has never happened.

I am tired now. I am tired of my own glitter. I pray, each night, for someone to challenge me, bust my myth, and ruin me; so I can finally be the recluse I was and was meant to be, and be in solitude like I dreamt to be. But it doesn't seem possible. The more I try to break free, you know, break back into the hated and disregarded human I was, the more people come in and tell me my 'worth'. The thing that grinds my gears the most, is that my attempts to show myself for who I am is interpreted as humility.

Humility. Bah, humbug!

There is no humility in trying to break free of the prison of people telling you that you're loved and but you don't know what they're talking about, because you know why they're saying that. There is no humility in knowing and failing to convey that you exactly what people mean and want. There is no humility in being trapped by the monster of knowledge. There is no humility in being ***Sahadeva***. It's a curse.

Until one fine day, at a certain restaurant, a woman looks at me. And she looks right through me.

She recognises that all my actions as an act, all my faces as a mask, and all my words as art. She knows what I mean when I say 'I know'. She knows what I mean when I say 'you won't understand'. She knows she can do it. She knows she can break me. And she is calling me closer, to end me, finally.

After years, ages, millennia; it seems, that I feel unsettled. Unnerved. After ages it seems like someone can find faults in me, and can not only see them but somehow knows them in vivid detail. And how I yearned for the challenge.

How I yearned to spew my bile at someone who disagreed with me. Someone so dull, who had lived their lives with no hills of self-choice and loud narcissism to die on, living by the known trails on plains of sacrifice, suffering and silence. Someone who just doesn't understand that life is indeed terribly short, but within its mundane boringness, it is insufferably long. Someone who never walked a mile with sorrow in fear of pain, and hence missed out on education of a lifetime. Someone who's never been around people so close to you that they're convinced that they know you, but in actual hard reality, they don't. Someone who has never been brushed with the basic sorrows of life, and here they are, trying to judge you for battling the most obscure of sorrows life has to offer.

I walk over to her, finally. She looks at me, with a quietly unquiet patience in her eyes. Her hands are folded in anticipation as if she knew I was coming. Her smirk was of one knowing heathen, but the heathen was me, not her. She was the anti-me. And yet..

That's when I realised, that this woman is different. She is someone who knows a pang. She is someone who has seen the hills I have and conquered them. Someone whose long life has been filled with reminders that it is incredibly short. She has the education of all the sorrows the life has to offer. Someone..who is she, just like me, as I am me, and thus is she.

She is the woman who made me the man I am. She is the woman who made the world love me. She's the woman, who I met, once again, who made me hate myself.

She is the woman whose lips once showed me the apocalypse.

In a Nightless Sleep

I am in one of those sudden downward curves now, where melancholy seems the pace of life; where the saxophone and the violin combine to make you cry; and the mind cries but the face smiles. The wish for rains has to be substituted with showers, the longing for warmth being compensated with tea, and the desire for a hug being put away with a pillow.

A feeling that has taken two and a half years to resurface, and it has finally made its home inside me again. This is a feeling that is all too familiar, yet each time it has a weird freshness to it, one which makes you severely unprepared whilst being awfully familiar with it. It's like meeting an old friend after years, and while the friend is the same, there's something different.

And that is when you realise that time is not a catalyst nor an inhibitor, it is a veil - a veil behind which flows the current of change and if you don't pay attention, you are either caught in the current or left behind. And while your attention to change is crucial, it is not enough. The powerlessness to fight the change is the epidemic of mankind - debilitating and mystifying. To be a passive observer as the world around you changes - building and crumbling, as one follows the other - and watching it happen helplessly is the defining challenge of our generation.

How to stay affected yet unperturbed, aware yet quiet, damaged yet scarless, and dying but alive, is the unholy grail.

And thus, for every smile I break, it reeks of a scavenged within; and as I close my eyes to sleep, my brain opens its eyes to see.

So long, Parthenon

The longevity of time. Yes, time. It sounds absurd when you think about it, and it should, as the phrase coins together a quality with its abstract. It brings into picture an upheaval of thoughts as you know them, because it puts a mirror in front of those very thoughts. It's like beating an inventor with his own machine, killing a writer with his own words, and questioning a god with his own powers.

Time, and the amount of it, if seen individually seems to be copiously scarce, or just not enough. Things move an inch a day and by the weekend they're lost. Or some presences are always around which never go by, even in years. Within that broken continuity, and around the chosen rupture, if certain revitalisations can occur, then you're in for a ride.

Because things change, with various levels of longevity. And that much anyone with a piece of life can understand - from the immobile tree to the wavering human. And within humans, even the least perceptive of all can percept change and act accordingly.

Trouble then, reeks from the minds of people who know a lot. Who've been blessed with Uriel's insights on patterns, who can link the sudden losses of the past to the epiphanies and revitalisations of the future. Those who live with presences - not necessarily with pieces of life but remnants of them, or more, or less - and drop them only to have them on their backs the moment they have a dilemma understand what it means to see beyond. And even if you try to show the beyond to people; some, or pitifully, most, can painfully see nothing beyond your finger.

Blessed with the curse of this knowledge, one is very astutely linked with a state of desolation. Desolation never comes in the way you think it will, or in the form you think it will. It'll come in the riches of people, or in the riches of gold, or in the riches of adulation. It'll come in the form of absent eyes, plugged ears and stuffed minds; or in the form of true poverty; or with a back full of holes. But desolation is for the one who knows, for one who knows is the one who forgoes. In whatever way possible.

Nevertheless, my roof is away, taken from what was once supposed to be a monument for the ages. It stands with a perimeter and pillars, which is a sinkhole of a prison. Oh, what it was. Oh, what it could be. Oh, what it would be if the roof was there. Sometimes the grasp varies - you think your pillars have collapsed and thus you've been crushed; but sometimes it's the roof that's off and the pillars stand there useless, with nothing to lift up. Both are desolation, and while one is claustrophobic, the other is the base of voluntary imprisonment.

I see no beauty. I do what I do, and yet people find it beautiful. They say it is actually. But they're wrong. I know this. I built it. I was inside it. Still am.

But someday I will step out. And walk far far away, away from the sunset. And if I turn, maybe I'll see what my Parthenon is now, and why the setting sun makes it look beautiful. And may I have the courage to say then,

"So long, Parthenon."

I'M SORRY, MIRROR

Is the demolition of one's self awareness deterioration or growth?

I was supposed to embark onto a new journey approximately two years ago - I was confident, self assured and knew my psyche and traits.

Or so I thought.

After about 700 days, I sit at about two in the night; battered, alone, lost, and defeated. I look into the mirror and don't recognise me. I don't know how the mirror will react when I try to talk to it. That always seemed to help, talking to myself, until I realised I have nothing to say, except sorry to the mirror. I've failed my own self within me.

I look at my shoulders and they seem bruised, from holding up weight or from extensive lending - I know not. I look at my eyes and I see a wail in there, a get me out plea which vanishes the moment I try to address it. I open my mouth to look at my tongue and it seems charred by the brunt of its heat. I look at someone I don't recognise, not because that person isn't me; but because I didn't know how I became that person.

It took hours and years to find myself. And it seems that in the past two years I've lost myself again. Where do I find myself? And how? How do I fish out that one wailing plea within me? How do I know what's happening with me when I have no idea what's happened to me?

At this point, this looks like a massive deterioration from what I was. People who knew me 4 years ago do not recognise me, and people who recognise me now do not know me.

And even if it is growth, is it a good one? How do I know it's not weeds? How do I convince myself that weed isn't all my soil can grow anymore?

When will the mirror say thank you to me?

Dragged Down a Memory Lane

I have quite a strong dissonance with the term "walking down the memory lane."

Quietly, in the general context, it is used for any form of reminiscing, remembering, recalling and reliving times and experiences one has had earlier. By its absolute etymology, it's a fine enough phrase in itself.

I have a problem with the way it has progressed through the years, as if memories are something stored in a locker which you can access at any time by logging in. Certain ones are - deeply etched and fairly recent ones to be precise - but most memories, in my experience, exist in a dormant state until a trigger livens them up.

And thus, you don't "walk" down a memory lane. You suddenly feel something and now you're in a particular lane of the city of memories associated with that feeling. You spot familiarity and the environment around you morphs into a different memory lane, reenacting that familiarity. Memory lanes either surround you unexpectedly, or memory triggers kidnap you and dump you into one.

And for someone like me, it can be a huge inconvenience. I like to know where I am going and which lane I am in, and sudden appearance of the labyrinth of memories can be a huge disruption. Imagine you're focused on one thing and a sudden trigger drops you at a fresh new memory lane - killing all efficiency, work rate and sometimes even progress. And then, when you're blank, or you need a distraction, memories refuse to pop up; as if you're stuck at the door without having the key. I have a problem with the insinuation that memories can be voluntarily triggered. So far, that has not been the case with me.

And the even more frustrating thing is that triggers are so well cascaded and hidden, that the room you have lived in for your life has concealed triggers taking you to memories you thought obsolete. Like finding a key while cleaning up your room.

Very, very much like finding a key while cleaning up your room.

I hadn't seen that key in years, and yet I recognised it in a jiffy. I knew where to put it in, and as keen I was for opening an unopened drawer for years, I as equally apprehensive.

I slowly put the key into the drawer, and forced it open somewhat. Pulled it through and I was laid on highways of memories.

Two magnetic keychains which when joined would spell "best friends forever." And I realised that whenever as a young boy I'd plan on gifting the other half to someone, that friendship would be dead. Ironically, a "best friends forever" keychain became a stark call out years ahead about my inability to maintain friendships.

A small thread, with a couple of small beads still around it. The friendship band tied to my wrist in 9th grade by my school crush. Things ended rather awkwardly, and the thread now represents the other painful strand of my school life.

Badges from many of my successfully completed youth leadership camps. Pang here is I've lost contact with all of the people I met there, the last and most painful bridge being burned a couple of weeks ago. Those badges are now a stark reminder of a "leader" who couldn't keep his pack.

Images with my work on them, cut and created by someone who believed in me and wanted to stay around me, and yet I pushed her away. An excruciating mark of my failure of appreciating people in my life.

I looked at all of these. That drawer, unintentionally and subconsciously had become a dump yard of stuff with memories which mark my failure in dealing with humans. It was a drawer with proof of my social failings.

I stared at the drawer's insides. I realised what I had to do.

I went and fetched the watch which was now too painful to look at, forget wearing it. And I put it in the drawer, as the newest souvenir of my failure with people.

ROMANCE

In Lots Of Vehement Emotions

The setting was perfect. The mild breeze over the vast blue lake was rustling the canopy of the tall trees around the terrace of the lakeside restaurant. The wooden bridge connecting the restaurant and the far side of the lake sat in the periphery like the finer details of an artist's masterpiece - greatly intensifying the overall beauty. The sky was a palette of yellow, orange and red, with the sun moving away to mark the onset of a memorable and gratifying evening.

Everything had to be perfect, and I reiterated that to the manager multiple times. He assured me with such competency that it almost settled my jitters. I took a deep breath, tried to calm myself down when the manager said with a twinkle in his eye, "Sir, she's here."

I turned, and there she was. Dressed like a dream in motion, she walked with the grace of a queen, yet she seemed to carry a carefree hop betraying the child within her she chose to share only to some. The bashful smile on her face didn't help her cause, as the entire place arranged itself around her. Nothing seemed to contain her, yet you could find her in every small part of my being. As I looked at her approaching me, the manager and other people faded away; the noises around quietened, and we were alone. Alone in that magnificent setting, just me and her.

"I could look into your eyes,
Until the sun comes up,
And we're wrapped In light and life and love.
Put your open lips on mine,
And slowly let them shut,

For they're designed to be together oh.
With your body next to mine,
Our hearts will beat as one,
And we set alight,
*We're afire love!"**

I still remember how it all began, she being the apex with me being the base; she was the flower the florist kept for his beloved while I was the one never sold. It sometimes happens that the ladder turns into a circle, bringing two ends of a spectrum together which gives a rather interesting image. I found myself closer to someone many dreamed to be in the vicinity of. Talks, sharing, aid, advice, support, infatuation, addiction - all followed. I cannot say when did the emotion develop; maybe it just clicked into existence the same day we met, like one of those secret treasures in video games that you desperately need but you don't know you needed it. Keeping an eye on her whenever she was around transitioned from my pass time to my habit. The feeling of warmth that spread through when she smiled at me, and the utter dread of having displeased her greatly after some erroneous incidents led to the realisation - that I had dropped into the mythical abyss about which the writers penned, the poets wrote and the singers sang. I felt a new lease of life, a new direction to heed my boat into, and my heart had a new found outlook wherein the world was richer, brighter and happier. The ficklest of creatures had fallen prey to the most savage of predators, the lightest feather had dropped from the dove and landed on me. Years and years of hitherto unknown bounds had been broken by carnage, and I got a freedom I didn't know I could have.

"So you can keep me,
Inside the pocket

Of your ripped jeans,
Holdin' me closer
'Til our eyes meet,
*You won't ever be alone!"**

I never knew the onset of a 'relationship', it just seemed that we unlocked each other - two complete souls finding their complement. We were both each other's pillars, hands that clasped which would be impossible to separate in the fiercest of storms. She dug me out of my muddy waters, replenished me when I thought I was drained and made me believe in myself. Piece by piece, she took the pain to rebuild the shards of a broken soul, taught it that the world blossoms when the heart leaps, and that every night, however dark, has an end. She taught me that a fish cannot drown alive, and that a bird cannot afford to be afraid of heights. Inherently, we both taught each other the valuable lesson - to give everyone importance but to set only the choicest few as priorities.

"Loving can heal,
Loving can mend your soul.
And it's the only thing that I know (know),
I swear it will get easier,
Remember that with every piece of ya,
*And it's the only thing we take with us when we die."**

We sat there, she beaming away, and I merely comprehending her the way a child watches on at their heroes. I could listen to her speak all night, all day, all year, until I ceased to exist. She made me feel high, intoxicated me to the level no amount of drinks could. She put her hand over mine, and raw current passed through my body. She talked, I listened.

I reasoned, she objected. The fact that we could brew up the most meaningless conversations amidst the most intellectual debates made us uniquely us. But more so, we could share moments of silence – beyond the brash and impertinent notions of conversations – and still exchange tons of our talk. Her eyes had a spark that reminded me of the power she could wield, instantly smashing you into smithereens if you made a crime; yet they were deep and soft; she had the natural feminine kindness which would be exponentially enhanced when filled with yearning and desire.

She was a source of light, and I was the shadow. She was bright, illuminating, and I was dark, refrained. Yet we weren't like other lights and shadows, which ran out of fuel and things would be over. She was the sun, and I was there wherever she graced her influence. And in the night, when the world threatened to turn it's back on her, I would gladly be the moon to reflect her light and to show the world what it was missing out on.

"Oh you can fit me,
Inside the necklace you got when you were 16,
Next to your heartbeat,
Where I should be,
*Keep it deep within your soul."**

People often have perceptions of their better halves, and I certainly did – adjusting, remodelling and redesigning after each dent it received. Sitting with her, I silently wondered when did I ever perceive such a colossal piece of grandeur. Then I understood I did not, the more I observed her I added a new stroke on the canvas, a gentle chisel on the final features of my sculpture, making them nearer to reality. Little did I know that my perceptions were a mirage of myself and my wants, and she is the reflection of myself and my needs. She found me, I found her, with each of us still being us - just a little more familiar. That is the entire purpose of the eternal quest - to know us better via the heart and soul of a chosen one.

"We make these memories for ourselves,
Where our eyes are never closing,
Hearts are never broken,
*Time's forever frozen still."**

The sun had set, and the bright moonlight reflected across the lake, shimmering along its boundaries. We walked, hand in hand along the wooden bridge, silent, enjoying each other's company and taking in the beauty nature had decided to bless us today with. How I wished it would start to rain, but that would make things a little too perfect. At the end of the bridge, under a small lighted boulevard along the bridge, she abruptly came to a stop and turned to me. With a characteristic mischievous smile glamouring in the faint orange light, she put her arms around me and leaned in, and I was only willing to oblige...

"When I'm away,
I will remember how you kissed me,
Under the lamppost,
Back on 6th street,
*Hearing you whisper through the phone.."**

My eyes opened. It took me a few minutes to get my bearings and to grasp the fact that it was just a dream.

"Someday, man," I smiled to myself, reassuring my sighing heart. "Someday, we'll be there."

** Quote Lyrics from Ed Sheeran's "Photograph" and "Afire Love".*

To Her Ravaging Memoirs

I make into my quietude, and try to break the impasse with my heart. 'Is this a night, or I am merely shrouded beneath her hair? Is this a mere gust of wind or the smells of her? Are these mere chitterings of birds or they carry her message?' I ask, peaceful and sagely. Even though I know that it's not her, but this wretched heart is obstinate. 'She's here,' it beats. 'Here somewhere.'

Transitions and transformations play a crucial role in life. Little did I know my transition would transform me such.

I never thought it would be like this. I never thought I'd be in this situation, one I never perceived before. I never thought, that she would be there near me, around me but never for me.

Life has come to a standstill. Spending the hours by amidst the rampaging days, walking past roaring vehicles and chattering sounds; time seems to stretch and stretch. The world is always in a blur, and behind that blur, I can see nought but a face. That one, very face; the ghost of my desires lost and sentiments prickled.

She was beautiful. Of course, she was. Her fair face, her pitch black hair - strands of which often played on her cheeks, her distinct jawline, thin rosy lips, a cheery smirk and the mischievous fire in her gentle eyes were etched and carved into my soul the way the ancient people had notched their gods onto cave walls. Never to be forgotten.

I see her walk and prance around in her joy, dance in her music and sing her songs. Her voice swims around in my conscience, engulfing me into her scents and jerking me out quickly; leaving me breathless and gasping for more of her. I was her prisoner, tied by steel chains which I had no intention to break out of; she was my jailer, never giving me enough to believe she cared for me yet kept me alive, and I was deep into Stockholm Syndrome - or as the masters of words call it - love.

I sit at my window, staring past the horizon into oblivion, trying to bring myself back. Back from where, I know not. Back from whom, I want to say not. "Move on, move on!" they said. "Love can move mountains", they said. But when it all ends, try moving back the mountains, alone. Try retracing the path you took, the distance you travelled, alone, with the memories nudging you - gently at first, but as time passes the nudge becomes a knock, and then a whack and then a blow. I sold myself to buy her love. And then I began to loan myself some life to live, and now I'm devoid of both - me and my life.

Late into the nights, I sit wide awake; recalling the feel of her touch and the smell of her hair when she hugged me, echoing her words as they were once addressed to me, and finally saying the words I wanted to then. There were a million things in my heart. A million things my brain failed to articulate. A million things lost in translation. All I ever wanted to do was be there for her. I wanted to be the one she searches for when she is nervous on the stage. I wanted to be that one person she runs to, to celebrate her victories. I wanted to be the solitary call she dials when she needs someone deep into the night. I wanted to be the one who made it all right in the morning. I wanted to be the ointment on her wounds and the bringer of shy smiles on her face. But mostly, I wanted her to be the one to tell me, "It's okay, I understand," when I needed it the most.

I have forgotten the hours I spent listening to music that splashed every inch of her on my face. It is a curse; I cannot cry. I am thirsty for my tears, which I pray will lighten her grip on me. But the drops won't come, and anguish is all that is left.

The heavens weep for me though. The rain that poured once carried her essence to me which I sheathed in, hid in. The rain that pours now still carries her essence which now tears me apart, one sense at a time.

The grey flashback brings me a memory, served with bitter and sweet sauces. An image, a moment, a still that caught us both doing things we loved most. She sat, playing with her pup and laughing out loud - the same laugh that was my favourite music once and the same laugh that leaves me wistful now. She was doing what she loved - living her life to the fullest. I was there beside her, watching her and smiling. I was doing what I loved, feasting my eyes and filling myself up with her. I still remember the walk that we took after.
'What is it, that you dream for? That if you could, you would magically like to have at the end of today?' she asked.

You, I thought.

'Myself,' I answer her now. 'Give me back to me,' I say aloud.

I walk. I talk. I learn and I laugh. I live - yes I do. I am a functional machine trotting out on a daily basis doing my chores. I haven't let myself into a swamp of immobility and uselessness. But even as yet, more and more as I try to breathe myself a new spirit, she comes in as a whiff of sweet fragrance. Day to day aspects lead me to her - from my early morning coffee to my late night tuning. I look into a future without her, and she pulls me into the past with her. Bittersweet yet, she makes me dive into a sham future of me and her, and of what-could-have-beens. She cannot be cut from me, nor can I just discard her like an old, childish wish. I must accept this one thing to sustain: moving on into the future doesn't mean losing the past.

I sit and write this, only to share what a rampage the monster named love can go to. I hold no grudges. Only the lovers know the kind of drug love can be, leaving you breathless and asking for more. Only the broken know the thrills of burning in the fires of Cupid, and only the survivors give you verses and portraits which transcend through time, true and beautiful. To all those who know what it is and how it feels, and for all those who know someone such. Love makes people do things they never thought they would. Some pick up the sword, some the pen. Some embrace the light, some dissolve into the darkness. But some, they just love.

WAIT FOR ME TO COME HOME

I scanned the surroundings. There was not a soul in sight.

I quietly walked towards her courtyard, deep into the chilly night, treading on the pavement as much as possible so as to avoid suspicion from possible nocturnal eyes. I trace the boundary, and jump inside the lawn just below her window.

Now comes the difficult part, to get her attention. Of course, I could have texted or called her, but being an old fashioned guy I did the old fashioned thing, I whistled. Not the best idea I have ever had, as the neighbour's dog went into a barking frenzy.

As I waited for that wretched dog to calm down, I re-theorized why I was there. There was only one answer to that.

I was there for her.

She was magic. She lived and breathed magic, magic which captivated me the moment I had seen her. The bold, carefree walk; the fierce and stubborn eyes, and the quick wit had me dangling on her entrails. But I stayed away. I had to go.

"So you should know this love we share was never made to die,

I'm glad we're on this one way street just you and I,

*Just you and I.."**

The dog quietened. I decided to throw some small pebbles on her windowsill. I threw a couple and waited. Pelted a few more, and waited. After what it seemed like an eternity later, she opened the window and looked out.

I grinned and bowed.

I expected her to squeal, jump in joy and come down running. Instead, she rolled her fingers around her temple, mouthing, *'Have you lost it?'*

I guess that is why we loved each other. Neither of us were sure what we'd do next.

Now that my expectations of how this night was supposed to go were thrown out of the window, I waited in jittery anxiety.

I remember when we discussed love. 'Do you know a synonym for love?' she asked.

'Um, affection? Desire? Endearment?'

'Do you believe that though? Do you believe that affection, desire or endearment or any other dictionary synonym actually encompasses in entirety what the word love means? Do they have the ability to trigger ten thousand different images in ten thousand people but still invoke the same feeling in all ten thousand hearts? Do they have the same charm?' She paused, 'The fact is, my grammarian,' she finally said, summarising, 'that there is no synonym for love.'

And how true she was.

"The more I know of you is the more I know I love you,

And the more that I'm sure I want you forever and ever more,

And the more that you love me, the more that I know,

Oh that I'm never gonna let you go,

*Gotta let you know that.."**

She tiptoed out of the back door, and as I saw her approaching me, I saw a mix of apprehension and worry on her face, masking utter delight and affection. I could have bet my life that her brain was planning on berating my sanity out while dropping down the stairs, but her heart appreciated my cheek and old fashioned romanticism.

She comes, and I prepare to hug her, to lift her. With a sly grin, I open my arms a little, as she completely ignores my gestures and lays a firm slap onto my cold cheek.

We stand there, staring at each other with my palm on my stinging cheek and her fists clasped firmly right by her side. Full ten seconds later, she hugs with twice the ferocity as the slap. I hug her back and lift her up, finally united, into the night, me and her. I hear a stifled sob, and I felt a little more guilty for being away, and to tell her to be strong once more.

There we stood, reunited, adrift from what anyone had to say or think. We completed each other, adding to what we had. That's the way love is, it adds an extra range to everything, making you revel in new boundaries of happiness, sadness, anger and despair. That is the true beauty of it - the fact that love isn't fair or noble in its nature - it's just that the nobler aspects are worth it more.

"And when the stars are shining brightly in the velvet sky,

I'll make a wish send it to heaven then make you want to cry..

The tears of joy for all the pleasure and the certainty.

That we're surrounded by the comfort and protection of..

*The highest powers. In lonely hours. The tears devour you.."**

She was the free spirit you thought only existed in fables. I'd promise to give her the most exquisite date and she would ask for a book reading night with her head in my lap. I would ask her what flowers she wanted and she'd take me dandelion picking together. I would ask for a piece of her and she would give me her all.

I drifted back to us discussing love. 'Thousands of times you may have heard the phrase 'I love you',' she said. 'Can you tell me which word is the most important in it?'

'Easy. Love.' I answered.

'Why?'

'Its the emotion! The deed of loving that makes this beautifully simple sentence the most exchanged in the world! The realisation, the feeling, the sentiments upon sharing the message.. the most important word is love!'

'What if I say that love is nothing without the loved? A lover can't love anything if there is nothing to love. Love doesn't exist if there's nothing to love. You know, it's the presence of something - attributes or flaws or anything - that makes it viable, substantial and capable of being loved. So the most important word in 'I love you' is 'you', not 'loved',' she said with a triumphant smirk.

If I could, I could have fallen in love with her, again, in that very moment. But I chose not to. Not because she wasn't the one, but because she was too free-spirited, and I was yet to find my spirit.

So we lay underneath the starry sky, jumping the lawn fence and into the open fields behind her house. We let the silence talk and shared our words by rubbing each other's hands. I could have spent my entire life there, with her, beneath the sky. I wasn't afraid of a thing, wasn't worried about anything, simply because she was there, with me, beside me.

"I wanna stand with you on a mountain,

I wanna bathe with you in the sea.

I wanna live like this forever,

*Until the sky falls down over me..."**

They say if you haven't loved, you haven't lived.

But I've found that if you haven't lived, you surely don't know what love is. Living is to love as the night is to the starry sky – you can't have the latter without the former. If you don't love yourself, you can't love anybody else.

I loved her. I loved her with all I could give. But I knew I had more to give for she gave me much more. So I had to live more, to give her more.

She said softly, '*Are you gonna stay?*'

This was the part I feared the most. She had been so brave and valiant, to be what she was when I knew I was an integral part of her being, yet so far away from her. Maybe I will never get what she's been through. I also knew, that if I asked for more she would definitely give me more – the marvellous woman that she was. But it would also crush her a little more.

I had to go. Once more. One last time. And soon. Dawn was about to break. I told her that, honestly. This was our relationship. The kind of relationship where we put down our needs of being superior, where we sketched out the fake promises and presumptuous acceptance, where we stopped being something we weren't. We were in a relationship where we were us, me and her, true and honest.

She took it well, but her eyes had the sadness that made me feel guilty of the deepest kind. I had to do something, to make both of us feel a little better.

'I love you like the sea loves the land, dear,' I said. 'Sometimes I attack your peace and drown everything you have. Sometimes I pat along on your feet. Sometimes I am mellow for you to bathe in me and sometimes I am in my own tune, and you have to sit and watch me. But darlin', that's how the sea loves. The sea also goes away, only to come back. But worry not, hey, because when I am away, look for me, for I'll leave a mark behind.'

She looked at me, and our eyes met. And we kissed, ferociously, so that we could remember the taste until we finally do unite once and for all. There, arms in arms we were one, and maybe if there was supposed to be no tomorrow, we knew we will always have this moment. We kissed, and the universe melted into her scent, and I had nothing in my mind and nothing but her in my heart.

As I began to leave, she held me back, hoping I'll say goodbye.

But I couldn't do it. Goodbyes are not my thing.

I know our love will endure. I know we will be there someday. I know, that our love lives on.

I step closer, clasp her face in my hands and whisper,

'Wait for me to come home.'

"I'm never gonna say goodbye,

Cos I never wanna see you cry,

I swore to you my love would remain,

And I'll swear it all over again..

I'm never gonna treat you bad,

Cos I never wanna see you sad,

I swore to share your joy and your pain,

*And I'll swear it all over again!"**

** Quoted lyrics from "Swear It Again – Westlife" and "Truly Madly Deeply – Savage Garden".*

Who Is 'She'?

The train shuffles along rapidly, with the dying sun creating beautiful tapestries while intermingling with the clouds. The strong hues of yellow and crimson are taking over the gradually vanishing remaining traces of blue. I put my temple on the window glass and fittingly, flag off a train of thoughts.

I close my eyes, and I realise that I can see more now. Putting in the dormant earphones, I could listen to many things even more clearly. I try to block every sense I can control, thus liberating a hitherto unknown treasure of space and time insinuated by the subconscious and picked up by the unconscious. As often, every once in a while my heart decides to join in my odyssey; and then the night becomes the day, sleep is left unneeded and the world has only us – me and her.

She walks with delicate poise, soft enough for you to never guess where she is going but strong enough to travel miles. Sometimes, she betrays a carefree hop, but it's quicker than a flash of lightning. Her verve is infectious enough to revive a dead soul. Her smile reverberates around, radiating warmth in her vicinity. Her eyes are full of kindness and brightness that shows you what you're dealing with. Her laugh makes you feel like treasuring the joke that tickled her if you can remember it while looking at her laugh. Her hands are as gentle as possible, yet have the dexterity and firmness that portrays hard work. Her touch is a soothing force which can simmer down my storms.

Yet I don't know how she looks like.

Her patience is a matter of great envy, like magically still water which refuses to be disturbed even if you throw large rocks into it – it would somehow take the rock in and be still. Her words are crafted with utmost heed, thought about and weighed in. Her talks can silence my raging rumination, solve my mammoth muddles and settle my angsty anxiety. Her voice, when she lets out her sagacity, is as supple as silk, but clear as a raindrop. To drive her point home, she looks straight into my eyes, and it sends a jolt which not only unties all the knots I have, but makes me feel sheepishly dunce for not seeing how simple things actually are. She reminds me, time and again, that success is lonely, rather than loneliness is success.

Yet I don't know what she sounds like.

Maybe she is the one person I know I need, but I don't know whether she needs me. And there's a fair chance she will never need me, or that my need for her is greatly substantial. She's the one who tapers my obtuse stubbornness, handles my bratty huffs, and manages to throw open my windows of constraints and let some fresh air in. She's the one who takes me to places I don't want to and making me see why I miss out on a lot. She takes the resolute bull-headed blockhead in me and throws me into her sea of openness, trying to teach me how to swim.

Yet, I don't know what she lives like.

She takes me to walks, hand in hand, along the river banks and on the beaches. We stroll around on the wet grass in the mornings, lay on them in the night and gaze at the stars. She rests her head on my shoulders, and I stay motionless for I don't want to disturb her. She slides her arm into mine when I'm down, and locks fingers with mine. She hugs me for fun, or at times to take me into her, with her smells and her freshly washed hair. And then, finally, she kisses me voraciously to shut me up.

Yet, I don't know what she feels like.

I think I am in love. I'm in love with the very idea of her. I'm in love with the unhealthy dependence I have on her. I'm in love with the very notion that she's around me, within me even if I don't know who she is. I'm in love with my obsession of her love. Maybe she is the only one who can love me the way I want to be loved. Maybe she is the only one who understands my love.

I don't know where she is. She could be here, right now, in front of me, looking at me while I enjoy my reverie. She could be on this very train. She could be at the next station. She could be the one reading this.

Or, I could never see her. She would never know me. She would never read this, never realise that I think of her, so highly or such vividly.

Maybe I will never meet her.

Maybe I *will*.

And when I do, I'll know.

To Us, Who Couldn't Be

To;

Us;

Who Couldn't Be.

There are little things in life that justify being quaint, particularly in this racing world. Yet, there still remains room for a good, old fashioned letter, particularly in circumstances like this; where none of us knows what to say but have a lot to convey. I don't hope to speak for you, and while I can only talk about me, I do think you are not very far off from what I have to say, so it eventually borders onto 'us'.

What we were is not what we are, that is clear. To be fair, our versions of what we 'were' don't match anymore, and I am surprised we managed to spend what time we could in the way we could.

Things went wrong. They went wrong in a manner I had epitomes of nostalgia associated with. I tried to say, there were times when I could be absolutely sure what your next line would be; and what your response would be. Not because I know you that well, that's never a possibility in months of internet chats, but because our conversation had reached a point wherein I had a constant case of Déjà vu, at almost every word, sentence and paragraph.

The déjà vu was as powerful as any. They brought back a notion of, 'here we go again'; and 'I should have seen this coming'. A certain feeling of the writing is on the wall and me being unable to notice it hung around my neck like a noose gradually being tightened, a noose which wouldn't kill me but would stop tightening at just the moment of extreme discomfort and breathlessness. And unfortunately, the marks of my previous escape from the noose were still a little raw.

There were things I couldn't explain, there were things you wouldn't understand, and there were many things you thought you understood but you didn't. And I don't blame you for it. I, for instance, am no one to go around blaming people. Things you couldn't understand were things I hope you never understand, because to understand them you need a certain experience to empathize, and I wish you never have those experiences. Then again, you have dealt with someone living with the repercussions of those experiences may have given you a certain curiosity, but please don't go about being Pandora who can't resist the temptation. Coming back to the things you wouldn't understand, again, it is not because you didn't have the ability to understand, but because you didn't have the will to accept them in their crudeness. You saw beauty in ruggedness and good things in bad, which I admire, but they were just not that. It is in these differences of experiences and understanding that a chasm opened up, and since I knew how wide it can be and futile it would be to try and jump across, I decided that it would be wise to say it quits. It wasn't the most morally upright decision, but it was one which kept both - you and me - safe. Maybe you do not get how this keeps you safe, but just by keeping you from jumping I hope I prevent you from burning into the fires beneath.

I appreciate what you've done, what you've said and what you've sent. I have never been a good receiver, either of good things or bad, so I just accept things with a customary thank you for everything. Since you had refuted the 'thank yous' I sent, I had no idea how to respond - for once I was out of words. I then decided to continue the conversation at my own peril, lack of sleep and discomfort. I appreciate the counselling, the praises and the credits.

In time, I hope you accept and respect my decision. It may feel that I wronged you immensely, and it may as well be true from where you're stationed, but just remember, if I did not leave the string we held I would drag you into a quagmire of stuff you don't deserve to be in.

In any case, if you need me desperately, I'll be there. And I will remember you.

Thanking and wishing you well;
Funadrius

Love Again

The elevator pings and I get in, a little dazed.

It was a day normal as any, typing away furiously at the keyboard, one eye on at the corner glass cubicle; with an extreme focus on the blinds.

It was boisterous, how the entire floor would straighten up with a start the moment the blinds were taken off; and how the collective entropy of the area would increase the moment they were drawn.

I was always focused on her, and then on the screen. It was easier to catch glimpses of her when the cubicle was watching, for there were no disturbances, distractions, or fear of getting caught by my fellow colleagues.

It was a heart-throbbing pastime, watching her as she prowled about and purposefully penned things down; and smoothly transition to the screen via a smiley chat on the phone. Her focused face would be tread on by a solitary lock of shiny black hair, whose audacity annoyed me. Then after a long stretch of work, she would relax, untie her hair, scrub her scalp and just lay back, breathing deeply. Just as you begin to think she's fallen asleep, she bustles into activity and I realise I've been watching her for far too long.

"I see you walking through the door;
but won't you look across the floor!
I've got to tell you how I feel,
*Oh baby you're the only one for me!"***

Lunchtime was when you'd see her at her social best, and me at my anti-social best. It took about fifteen minutes - about one-third of the allowed lunchtime - to locate a seat with a clear view of her. Until, one fine day, we sat on the same table, face to face.

That was today.

The elevator door opens, and I walk towards the bus stop, constantly replaying the chat during lunch time - the courteous smiles, interested nods, quizzical eyes, sharp ears and that one hysterical laugh I managed to extract. The fact that I managed to speak, let alone engage her in conversation still amazes me.

"Hey ya, I wanna be closer to you,
Hey ya, I need to be closer to you.
I got to tell you how I feel,
*Oh baby you're the only one for me!"***

No, no, no. I mustn't delve on it. This is all an unwanted déjà vu, and suddenly the conversation of today clashes with the many I've had before.

"Wasn't it only a couple of years ago, when you were smitten to the core?" I ask myself, sternly. "How did that end up?"

But this is different. It feels different.

Or does it? *Is* it?

It always begins like this, from corners of your eyes to a touch-and-go encounter with her, then a coffee and then the exchange of numbers, only for her to tell you via text that either she has a boyfriend, is engaged, or worst of all, isn't interested in you. The closing of doors via circumstance doesn't hurt as much as being told you never really had a chance. Probably it is because of the wretched hope that somehow, in some twisted way the doors may barge open with her in a wedding dress darting through and embracing you, movie style. It is that hypothetical chance of minimal redemption that keeps a little flame burning, and if it is not put out it can char your heart black.

"You can not keep your eye off her," somewhere within me something retaliates as I rest my head on the bus. "And do not lie, there's something about this woman that we both know is different," it argues.

Sure she is. There is an adherent maturity that seeps out in everything she does, as if she would understand every action you'd do, be it a gracious kindness or cold-blooded murder. She also portrayed the boldness and tact to call you out and tuck you in jail as well for the murder, while telling you she understood why you did it. No wonder the cubicle was hers.

"Crossing on my fingers,
Baby don't let it go,
This feeling I'm getting,
I haven't felt it a lot,
I surrender myself to you,
*The soul I want you to know.."***

But that was my exact worry; such wonderful women are rare, difficult and challenging for their own merit. There's a gulf between us, primarily defined by the steps between my desk and her cubicle. She's a classic, unique portrait from the renaissance, and I am a scrawl by an amateur.

And as for the past, I had sworn that never will I ever fall in love again, and if I ever do slip, it will remain buried within me. For nobody needs a needy love. That's the way I loved, and being unapologetic about it came at the cost of acceptance and receiving love. I resolved that I may be miles into the abyss of love, crushed beneath tonnes of affection, but it would never come out in any way. No bouts of frustration will give away my need for love, nor would any sweet persuasion charm out the dark secret. As easily as I failed in not ever being in love again, I was determined to not fail in the second part of my oath.

As I unlock the doors of my apartment, I fall into another reverie. I imagine her with me, in this very apartment, cosy beneath the same blanket watching movies. Or maybe me with my head in her lap, listening to her read out a poem. I imagine us cooking together, and chatting deep into the nights with her coffee and my tea. I imagine quarrels over the cushions and the decor. And my heart skips a beat at her trying to console me. I wish that there would be a time when I would enter the apartment awash in candlelight, and we would have a romantic dinner together. And I even dared to see myself down on one knee, at a beautiful lakeside restaurant, and she whispering 'yes.'

"I'm never gonna live without you baby now,
You're the only one who'll always be my fantasy,
You're the only one to make me reach my ecstasy,
I don't want nobody else but you,
*I'm loving you; I'm loving you!"***

No. I cannot get pulled into a hypothetical possibility which will never come into fruition. I rush and splash my face numerous times with cold water. The chill takes away my breath momentously and brings me back to my senses.

As I wipe my face, I think.

Apparently, I think a lot about love, which can only mean I have been terribly unloved so far. Despite that, I believe that with every breath I take, I fall in love a little bit more, with whom or what may not be defined. And within that, on she comes to take my breath away, countless times. It is all about the times when your heart has skipped a beat, and if in some way if you can count the beats that you skipped in love, you haven't loved enough.

Enough. It's time to finally quit this mirage. I turn to music, hoping it will be my saviour as it always is.

I lay on my bed, turn on my music. '*Phir Mohabbat**' begins to play.

I sigh and smile. There's no escaping cupid today, I realise, and give in.

* *Love Again*

** *Quoted Song Lyrics from "Hey Ya – Karthik Calling Karthik", "Mera Jeena Hai Kya – Aashayen", and "Sarphira Sa Hai Dil – Luv You Mr. Kalakaar."*

My Nights, His Sleep

It's three in the morning. I stare at the ceiling, gazing at the dark nothingness, perfectly awake. Sleep had not bothered to knock on my doorstep, or rather, it was kept at bay by nothing significant.

If only I could believe what I just said.

Not the fact that I was wide awake, but my meek attempt to pass him off as insignificant. His significance is something I never could define, but somehow always felt reliant on. He wasn't vocally and visibly important, but he was essential when it was dark and quiet. He was the Batman to my other Harvey Dents.

That analogy jolts me up, and I decide there and then; that you must know this. You must know about the Batman who made me his Gotham, and who'd have loved seeing me make these analogies.

He was an unusual fellow. He brooded into the nights and acted during the day; slow and cautious, but firm. He was ostensibly arrogant, they said, but a certain unrelenting confidence backed up by reasoning is often taken as arrogance by the rash and intuitive. And we happened to cross paths by chance, literally. Two frenzied readers, imaginative people who imagined nothing less than the chance of love with a dose of occasional love by chance; bumping into each other at the romance section of a book fair. He seemed to be a devout reader, geeky round glasses and unkempt hair and beard, with a carefree feel of carelessness around his actions. He picked up books quickly and put them down even more quickly, as if he could scan the chapters in the flick of an eye. Until, of course, he found that one book that catered to his needs, and started reading it at the stall, right there and then; only to be reprimanded by the seller to either buy it and leave or keep browsing. He was so engrossed in reading that the curt rebuke startled him, and a giggle escaped my mouth before I knew it. He turned, and realised that he was being watched, turned beet red and smiled sheepishly. He hastily grabbed the book, and carried it to the cashier, expertly hiding the title from view.

Ah, the joys of catching boys enjoying their unadmitted pleasures!

The roll of the dice showed six, and we ended up meeting each other five more times in the same fair, until I decided to shatter the ice. A coffee treat wasn't very tempting for him, but tea softened his stance. Tea made him slip out details. His restless demeanour terminated at his eyes, still like an icy lake in mid-winter. Yet, there was a fire behind the ice, which could either melt him or burn me. And I decided to poke the fire.

He could write as he could read - heavily and excellently. His writings made me think of the things he had gone through, the fears he had overcome and the scars that shone on his soul. The way he trapped his emotions into words and laid out a maze for you to get lost in, you almost didn't want to come out of it. Looking back at the things he wrote reminds me about this piece of wisdom, when he so nonchalantly uttered, "*Looking back is always difficult because there's hindsight, and hindsight is the mother of nostalgia, and the grandmother of regret.*" I could almost hear him say things he wrote. The strength he portrayed, the inspiration he shared and the creativity he spilt made me wonder what was hidden beneath his ungodly untidy hair.

Whatever he was, he was not just that. He had that one extra thing which drew your attention, yet he did incredibly well to stick to himself. He felt alone, torn between the choice of solitude and mingling. He was bold, opinionated and could use those opinions to barge through the mind of his opponents. Yet, there was a mildness, a type of kindness and sensitivity that surprised many, probably even himself. He thought of it as a vulnerability, given the pain it had given him. And I failed to convince him it was his real strength.

He was not many people's idea of companionship. We often talk about the seldom used, not the sharpest tool in the shed, but he was the tool sharper than others; kept aside because there wasn't a worker skilled enough for him. The brightest crayon in the box, seldom used because there wasn't a tapestry dark enough for him, and he had convinced himself that he'd only be useful if things were 'dark'. People would ask him for aid, and he would provide it and be off, away, to find other shades of darkness to kill. He was the friend they deserved, but was never the one they needed often, so they forgot him. Because he could take it, because he was a hero. He was a support in the shadows, a thankless soldier. The "Dark Knight" in the darkest of your nights.

He did a lot for me, and never waited for my thanks. It was then when I understood how unerringly evil his habit was, to not wait for gratitude. Gratitude is not properly understood. It is not something to be passed off as nothing. And the biggest wrongdoers are people and deeds that don't accept gratitude, for they demand indebtedness in return. The debt I took from him was immense, and I have no idea how to repay it.

It provides the greatest satisfaction to please the difficult to please, to extract love from the difficult to love, and to understand those difficult to understand. Such was he, but you could be sure that when he loved, he loved deeply. A drop of his love was so pure, that it would pierce through tonnes of hate. Such kind of love that feels like the burn from cold ice. Love, that can only be met with fires that cool, maybe.

He taught me to fight. He told me to stand up for what I believe in. He convinced me that respect is earned, not demanded. He made me not let things go, taught that I shouldn't have to lower my gaze for someone to take pride in their unabashedness. He saw things in me I didn't, even if he refused to show them to me directly. He forced me to dig into myself, think, and understand what I was all about. And by the time I realised who I was.. he was gone.

How I wish I could talk to him once more. Oh, if only once!

What wouldn't I give for him to scratch his ear again when I confuse him and make him think! What wouldn't I give to see him run his hands through his hair every fifteen minutes! What wouldn't I give to feel his beard again!

How I wish I could hear him say again, "Fine! You're right!" when he doesn't want to argue anymore. I would walk to hell and back for him to make DC and Marvel jokes again, and tell him that I now understand them. How much do I want him to come and show me again, to tell me where I am wrong. How much do I want him to validate what I think, to run through what I plan. How much do I want him to ruin me once more, and break me into a thousand pieces from the hundred that I am, so that I can allow him to see more of me than anybody has ever before.

So there you are. Dawn is up, and I hope the shower will run him off my mind once again as it does to a lot of things.

But I know he will always be significant to me. Significant enough to think about him for nights and nights. They remain my nights, but my sleep is his.

The Shortest Night

The room was a mess. The curtains were askew along the windows, the cushions were lying helter skelter. The table was full of empty food bowls, wrappers and cans. Towels and clothings were spread throughout. The television was on, but I had set it on mute. On the couch she slept, peaceful and calm. She was here for a party and had crashed the night.

I sat across her on my chair, sipping on my cup of tea and watching her chest inflate and deflate repeatedly. Sleeping in an almost fetal position, she looked like a little girl. The wind from the fan swung the hair on her face. She clutched the blanket which I had draped on her when she fell abruptly asleep dearly. Her face carried a mild smile, like she was dreaming about beautiful things - things she loved. It was surreal, how that one body could be a splendid amalgam of craziness, weirdness, fun, maturity, responsibiity, humour and more. That one 8×4 feet couch held a little stardust, some dark sprinklings, some mild rays and a strong fire.

I did not know what she dreamt of. Maybe she dreamt of her love, or loves; plural as they must be. Or perhaps some happy memories. Even an implausible possibility? Maybe she saw a pleasant future.

Or maybe, she dreamt of her happiness at the implausible possibility of me as her love in her pleasant future.

No, that's just me hypothesising the plausibility of my happniess on the possibility of me being her love in her pleasant future.

I love her. There's no qualms about it. And she doesn't know it. At least, I think she doesn't. That's because neither have I let the floodgates open nor has she sought to swim in the waters I hold. That doesn't mean I haven't let a few drops out. They were more like the water that tops off a fully filled glass when moved, as compared to me letting it flow out.

She moves suddenly in her sleep, and tosses around into a new position. I watch her motionless with the cup of tea just near my lips; afraid to move or make any noise which may wake her up.

'**What are you waiting for?**' I asked myself as I finally get up and start preparing breakfast. There will never be a better opportunity than today, it seemed. Both of us, alone, over breakfast as the mild morning sun drenched my kitchen. Yet I knew I won't be talking to her about me.

Probably I was scared. It's natural to be. I wasn't scared of her being already in love with somebody. I wasn't scared of rejection. In fact, if she was happy, I could live with that and without her. I was scared of the fact that my two minutes of heartfelt talk may ruin what we have, whatever we have. That she may distance herself after that, or even worse, just cut loose. I could live with the regret of keeping my love in rather than live with the curse of the aftermath of my expression.

I wish love was as simple as it was when we were young – penned on the backs of our notebooks. Shaped via bollywood and other romantic storylines, I never realised the terrors of love before and the peace of it after heartbreak. If I still had a notebook I kept with me everywhere, I'd have to read it backwards; thanks to her.

Sleep had abandoned me all night, but not for the usual reasons. The root was the same, yet my heart couldn't formulate that she was there, in actuality, in my apartment; for the night. I told her to wait while I prepared a room for her, but by the time I was back she was dozing on the couch.

The horrible thing about love is that it makes you question your ethics, puncture your morals and duel your conscience. It would be awful to have her wake up seeing me watching her - but even though my brain refused, my eyes revolted.

It was the shortest night of my life.

Maybe my hitherto unsaid and unseen selfish motive was to have her approach me with her undying love for me. And I, with glee and jubilation beyond bounds would accept it and we'd be happy forever after. Now that I think about it, that would be great, even if it was even more implausible and unhealthy to ponder upon and expect.

As I checked the fridge for juice and milk I thought about the possibility of me asking her out in a couple of hours and she actually saying yes. Just the thought made me freeze at the kitchen door, juice carton in hand.

The sheer gloriousness of it hit me hard. Waking up to her beside me every morning, smelling her hair when she hugs me tight. Walking in the park with her grasping my arm and putting her head on my shoulders. Sitting on the park bench with my head in her lap, and she just casually stroking my hair as the mild breeze makes her long locks tickle my cheeks. Quibbling over mugs and cutlery, tops and shirts, dresses and blazers. Having an infinitely long indecision over what to eat for lunch, and ordering pizzas anyway. Fighting over that last slice of pizza, eventually eating it together. Devouring the same noodle until our lips meet. Sipping tea from each other's cups, making sure I sip from the same spot she did. Having crazy dates to the local fair, with she taking me to rides which scare the heavens out of me. Clicking her pictures by the small lake at the restaurant. Coming back home wild, intoxicated with each other. Feeling every inch of her body. Tracing my name on her bare back until she recognises it. Planning a surprise for her when she catches me red handed and asks me, 'What are you doing?' And I hastily and sheepishly reply, 'Nothing!'

I stood there, frozen, with a stupid smile on my face. The refrigerator was almost yelling loudly for me to shut the door, to no avail. It was then when her astonished voice brought me back to my senses,

'Uh, what are you doing?' she asked while rubbing her eyes.

I smiled sheepishly, rub my hand on the back of my head and said,

'Nothing!'

We Meet Again

"I'm – I'm not the same person that I was five years ago," she said.

I looked at her. There was the same set of dark brown eyes; her beautifully shaped jawline which was perhaps even more distinct now; same slender arms, one of which still had the silver quartz watch her mom gifted her; and a rather dull colour choice of clothes. She would seem the same to anyone who'd known her before.

Yet I could see some differences. Her eye sockets were a shade heavier than her cheeks, and her once restless, trusting gaze was now steely and fiery. Her hair, which she liked long, was shorter than usual. Once jet black and thick, her hair seemed a little thinned and betrayed a couple of white strands. Her knuckles looked bonier than before, and her skin whiter than before, which made me worry about she skipping her iron supplements. Her poise had changed, it portrayed strength which overshadowed her previously held mild joviality. It was as if she was constantly on her toes.

If she was a cinnamon roll then, she definitely looked like she had left it in the past.

When I had met her initially, I knew straight away that I was going to immortalize her. I knew that my pen would jot her down and prepare a sketch of her in the only way it knew – with my words. If I wasn't lucky, I would have to do with only a fleeting glance as inspiration. However, I was lucky. Very, very lucky.

Which may or may not have been a blessing.

You see, the moment I saw her, she birthed a range of verses and poetry within me. I knew that this woman was going to be the fodder of my pieces. I knew that she would make me get up from my bed at three in the morning because my heart had just shown me an imagery of her which I just ***had*** to write then and there. The catch was, what emotions would weave themselves into the writing. She could be the panache of requited love, or she could be the spiritlessness of love unanswered. The more I knew her the more I could craft, but the more I got of her the more direction our story would get. And then the direction would control the quill. I could imagine me and her entwined in a hug, but that hug could be of union or of farewell. And depending on how things panned out in reality, the subsequent piece would either make the reader giddy in the stomach or heavy in the eyes.

But here we were, years after the hug of farewell. During that time we had been subjected to the phenomenon of change, along with the responsibility of moving on.

Initially, it was just the change in the habit of each other. The first few days were the worst, when every small thing echoed her presence. Her scent was everywhere, her influence engraved on my days. As the days passed her essence slowly diffused, but never really went away. Her absence led to a decrease in her influence, and I learnt to do things for myself again. As the weeks passed by she turned into a reminder of the past I had. This was the buffer zone, wherein I felt I had moved on - only to see her picture on social media and drop back into her. I ended up checking her profile for hours, investigating every face in her pictures to overstating and trying to read between the lines of her posts - until I finally checked myself.

Then, as soon as I abolished her out of my days, she barraged into my nights - again. She popped up in one too many dreams, which would ruin mornings and the subsequent days. And then, months later, when I finally started 'living' without her, I thought I was through. Until I finally met her again.

The changes in my situation led to many changes in me - I stopped being dependent on the small things she brought into my life. I began doing things on my own, engrossing myself and engulfing her out. I spoke to people with greater cautiousness, which at times helped me out as it passed off as respect. I did not prod around, minded my own business, but never allowed someone to encroach. I was definitely not available. I grew up, I matured. I learnt pain, and learnt how to deal with it. I began to download older songs whose lyrics began to make more and more sense to me day by day. Soon, my playlist was only mine - it no longer was something universally praised. I became a better listener, probably because I feared talking more would make me let things out which should not be out. I became an empathizer from a sympathizer. I learnt how to defocus from a trigger. Soon, I started giving out advice at 2 AM calls instead of asking for it.

The day I would meet her again was the day I feared the most. The prospect of facing her again and telling her, probably untruthfully, that I had moved on from her was horrendous. What would she think? That I didn't love her enough at all? Or that my love is fickle and easily washed off? Another thing which scared me even more was if ***she*** had moved on? What if she refused to acknowledge me? Or worse, even refuse to recognise me? What if, she was still something to me, but I was nothing to her? What if, she has moved on so well that she's found somebody ***else***?

They say you have to face your worst fears. And that's what I did when we met again, by chance.

I could see some changes in her which were similar to mine. I saw some changes which were not, and I wished to ask her about them. And then I realised I don't have the right anymore. Nor do I have the permission, else she'd have asked me about the way I've changed. Instead we talked about the good times, and then after we were done we looked into each other's eyes. I did not back away, but she looked away exasperated. I realised I'd made her uncomfortable, and we awkwardly sat in silence. But there was one question that was nagging me ever since I had met her again, and I willed for her to look at me again. Reluctantly, she obliged, and the fact that we still possesed that telepathic connection made it worse - and gave me half of my answer. Nevertheless, I implored the question with my eyes, and this time, she stared right back, as tears formed into her eyes, which said without voice, "*Not yet.*"

I hope, for the sake of us both, that the "*Not yet*" doesn't change to "*Probably never.*"

Maybe we have differently aged, contrastingly matured souls now. Maybe we were in love but incompatible then, and we may be more compatible now as much in love, but probably not meant to be.

I pray, this is a case of "*Not yet*" over "*Probably never.*"

Whatever it is, but we respect each other's changes and take certain responsibility for it - to the extent that when she said, "*I'm - I'm not the same person that I was five years ago,*"

I replied, "**I hope so,**" and smiled.

A Drive of Love

The salty breeze parted my hair. The night sky was pitch black and had specks of white which seemed to be stars. The waves hit the rocks with aplomb, as I sat with legs crossed and shoulders slouched.

I looked into the horizon, towards the Mumbai skyline. The more I focused, the more lights appeared in the distance. The more I sought, the more borderlines of buildings and structures appeared. Until I blinked and they all vanished.

A few cold drops from a strong wave hitting the rocks below touched my face, triggering goosebumps. Goosebumps which required just an excuse to pop up I reckon. Ever since I was with her, they've been excited to jump out, much like an overenthusiastic puppy after locating its owner.

With her. These two words can mean so much; ranging from a mere companionship to everything beyond that. But beyond the influence of physical presence, something I haven't discovered yet exists an entire realm of presence; wherein we play, love, heal, and talk. We talk about things I haughtily assume people, in general, don't, we heal each other in a way I proudly presume we haven't before; yet we play in a simple way as almost everyone does. How do we love, though?

Love. What is love? Many, including myself, have been questioning that, and as I've pondered about it more I've realised that it means differently to every person. Some see love in bodies, some in the skin, some skin deep, some in the hair. Some within the heart, some in the soul, some in the scars, some in the mind. Some in the blocks, some in the barriers, some within the vulnerabilities, some deep into the fears, while some find love in the opposite of each. Brilliantly enough, none of those approaches are right or wrong, even though disagreements may arise. How does one love someone, or doesn't, is dependent on how one has lived, and even the most mundanely similar lives vary in the bitsy aspects of every day that are unique within the common.

The question then, is not how one does love another, as to how does one love oneself. Quite often, loving someone is the later stage of making them love themselves. It is not a noble take, at least not as noble as words may portray, it is inherently selfish. If one doesn't love oneself, there is no way he or she will able to love you. When it was said, 'to get love you must give love,' it didn't mean that you need to love someone to get love back. It was a hint, that you need to give them the blessing of loving themselves, to get the fruit of them loving you.

You want someone to love you? Make them love themselves, and that love will eventually find you.

Of course, you can only do that when you love yourself.

What does loving oneself mean?

Loving oneself is the simple and straight act of giving yourself what you'd give to someone you love. As humans, many of us have a tendency to either judge ourselves too harshly or too favourably. In either case, it leads to detrimental effects. The most valuable part of love is honesty, it is the mammoth block of ice beneath the tip of the iceberg that is love. Nothing in love strives without honesty, as from honesty stems the glorious aspects of love - trust, belief, faith, assurance and knowingness. And if you aren't giving someone you love your honesty, you aren't loving them, at least not yet. Give yourself some honesty before you give it to love, as that will mould you into a better person. And a better you is easier for you to love, and more capable to make others love themselves, and eventually more lovable in return.

Give yourself the same space to make errors you'd give to your loved one. Allow yourself the same forgiveness that you give to them. Take off steam from your own head just as you will take theirs. One of the greatest lessons she has taught me was to be me, while I constantly try to make her the best version of herself. Probably a little swap in approaches from time to time would be awesome.

Love is learning. Love is a path. Love is finding someone who is equal parts your complement and equal parts your polar opposite. You want to be with someone who, deep down, is just like you - you share the same values and beliefs, probably even favourite music and teams, you share the same outlook on life. But beyond that, you will want differences, for they are what you will talk about. You need differences to understand the other person better, and to grasp what makes them tick. It is the differences which will make you appreciate the seperate entity that the person is. And the differences are the factors that will maintain an element of surprise and excitement throughout.

It is both, however, the fact that you are similar yet different; two different entities yet intertwined into something bigger; that makes you appreciate the wonder that love is. Two wholes doubling up into a strength that shakes the world. A little dark in white and a little white in the dark - two human beings, one bond. Love.

I took a deep breath. The cool wind in my lungs seemed to freshen me up. Despite me being there alone, I knew I truly wasn't. I rarely am. Either I am with her or she is with me, and despite being miles away this makes sense. Sometimes she encroaches my thoughts, and sometimes I go to her. And very much like the Mumbai skyline from Marine Drive, the more I focused on her, the more I could see and hear her everytime.

And as the lateness of the hour dawned on me, I heard her tell me to go home and sleep.

Sure enough, came a ping, as I smiled and started walking.

Here With You

I sit on the bench, smiling into my phone screen, scrolling and reading the words I've already read millions of times before. I scroll up until I see that one text, and then remember the call that followed. As my eyes lose focus of the text and my mind drifts off to her voice, my smile turns into a grin.

I lay back, and stare up onto the ceiling. The station roof was intricately designed with metal beams and supports, and upon proper attention, you could see the symmetric and structured beauty of it. A train was standing in front of me, destined to take me momentarily away and yet eventually take me ever closer. Every inch that I move in the other direction takes away seconds from the time gap of rendezvous, and so I may be inches farther but I am actually minutes closer.

It had been a fantastic day. Fantastic due to ordinary moments extraordinarily transpired, not due to extraordinary moments in an extraordinary day. The beauty of a gradually transformed mundane is akin to a collection of dandelions - nothing of generic beauty or extraordinary, yet extraordinarily beautiful at times. The transition, or rather shift these days has been not the presence of somebody, as surprising as it may seem, but the sheer prospect of gratifying and intensifying the presence into the case of substantiation.

"A hundred days have made me older
Since the last time that I saw your pretty face.
A thousand lies have made me colder
And I don't think I can look at this the same.
All the miles that separate
Disappear now when I'm dreamin' of your face."

I get on the train, and I have secured my favourite seat. As I make myself comfortable, I realise that I have been ignoring my train journeys this year. They used to be a part of my romanticised fantasies, and while the fantasy has begun to furnish a little, the absence of trains in them was now bothering me. Fittingly, the moment I rested my temple beside the window as I always do, the train began to shower its resentment at me. I couldn't know whether it was an intention to punish me for my ignorance or just a very fervent welcome back - often the difference is like trying to differentiate between day to day Urdu and Hindi, only the knowledgeable can.

"So I finally have your attention, do I?" it questioned, sarcastically. "I used to be the hoarder of thoughts which you wrote about. What now, though? What do you write about now?" It complained. A sheepish smile didn't leave my face, and somehow it knew. "My chugs and tugs made you zone out so you could think," it whined, "and now you zone out my chugs and tugs so you can think about someone else? It's the night travel, boy, and there's only one thing on your mind. There's a dream in your eyes, and within that dream is someone, and there's this lack of loneliness I now sense, which renders me useless, isn't it? She's not here, but she's still here with you."

"I'm here without you baby
But you're still on my lonely mind.
I think about you baby and I dream about you all the time.
I'm here without you baby
But you're still with me in my dreams
And tonight girl, it's only you and me."

It was easy to talk to and convince the train, that today it wasn't about me ignoring its sounds. Today was about rediscovering the said sounds, and counting them as time ticks away. I've told the train about many a people coming and leaving, about the glories and disdains of life, and about how I have a habit of anthropomorphising things into personalities, and somehow even getting answers in return. I have travelled long cumulative distances with the train, and each time it tells me something different. The fact that now I have another source to tell me things I need, makes me wonder if I could ever repay the train for being there when I needed it; when it was, full of people but only talking to me, often as **she** does now.

But just as the way the train has taught me selfless love, as a very nod to that it will take me to and from, with and beyond her. And I know it will always be there for me – sometimes a little late, maybe, sadly – as I will be there for her.

"The miles just keep rollin'
As the people leave their way to say hello
I've heard this life is overrated
But I hope that it gets better as we go."

Yet the wait is hard. Not because I have to go through a great ordeal whilst the wait, but because I wish to do nothing and now I have to do not much while I wait. The wait is a pain when you have nothing on your mind – nay, nothing but the wait on your mind. An empty mind is the devil's workshop, and the expectant mind is a creative disaster. Creative, as humans are thus so creative that they create their own new problems, even within a cocoon of a self-chosen environment of favourable constituents. It is then I see how love can be a problem, despite it not giving me any pains. How it's tentative deadlines and pervasive presence (or sometimes the lack of it) leads to different notions of it. How love takes preys, makes people fall and rise, and thus belies itself.

I won't say I understand love, nor do I claim that I want to. I just *know* that it is love, and beyond that I know naught. I know that the distance that keeps us apart physically has somehow managed to bring us together in a way not possible. I know that probably she's there without me, but I am soon going to tell her to her face that I am always going to be,

here with you.

"Everything I know, and anywhere I go,
It gets hard, but it won't take away my love.
And when the last one falls, when it's all said and done,
It gets hard, but it won't take away my love.I'm here without you, baby,
But you're still on my lonely mind.
I think about you, baby,
And I dream about you all the time.
I'm here without you, baby,
But you're still with me in my dreams,
*And tonight, girl, it's only you and me."**

Quote lyrics from 'Here Without You - 3 Doors Down'.

I Will Meet You There

Somewhere far far away, beyond the realm of allure and distaste, exists a small bench. I will meet you there, to wipe away the clouds of doubts from your mind. We will sit there, beneath the very sky which refused to house you in the night and was tired of me staring at it desperately. We shall sit and look in different directions, thinking ten different things, and yet rounding up on similar tones. We shall sing the same songs in our mind, for I am a million times a better singer in my head. We shall gently move and touch each others' hands, sparking an emittance, like two different vines intermingling behind our backs as the sun sets.

Somewhere far far away, far from the highway of judgement, exists a small rickshaw. I will sit with you in it, and we will travel to the land of books. We will set on a journey that either of us planned, but neither of us will forget. We will tear past those very eyes which never saw us break but will glare as we try to join ourselves back together. We shall travel by lakes and buildings, plains and plateaus, and end at a bookstore in the hills. And on a small house between the hills, I will read words to you as you drift off to sleep, and wake up to a warm mountain sun on your face. As I walk out on the verandah, the sun greets me as it always does, with the contempt someone lonely gives to a person in affectionate company.

Somewhere far far away, above the smoke of who's whose, is a small canteen. I will meet you there, and we will have sandwiches. We will have a discourse none of us thought would happen in such capacity. We will marvel at the differences in our past, and then ponder about the similarities in our future - until one of us realises to live in the present. It is then we realise there exists nothing like the present, the second you mention as present is already in the past, and the next one will also be when you get to talk about it. We will then realise how pointless time can be, within eyes, within minds, and within souls. And as we live then, we realise that the present is nothing but something that is felt, as you feel time dawdling away. As we leave then, we understand that this night will forever be ours, as you feel the time running away.

Somewhere far far away, away from the land of loss, is a solitary Uber, I will take you in it, deep into the night, to liberate the fears in you. We shall move into the backseat, shuffle our playlists and play a song - one in particular which I had lost in the labyrinth of my mind. As it plays I put my head on your shoulder, and your humming vibrates within me. We gently breathe into that shared space, a warmth within the cold of the night engulfs us, with two vines perfectly wound perfectly and tightly, as the sun rises gently, announcing the dawn of us.

The night sky will then accept you with a smile, and the hilly sun will be friends with me again. The time will stop and the night will be ours, as the vines hold each other as tightly as ever.

Somewhere far far away, I will meet you.

I will meet you there.

Second Time Around

Life is nothing but a woven book of stories, linking together like an entangled chain. By the time you realise the complexity of its linkage, you're either at the end of the book or at peace with the mess. Ever so rarely does an effort to untangle life comes into view, yet there are hands that work furiously every day inside their own books, trying to make sense of the words, paragraphs, pages, and chapters. The nature of that effort is such that the outcome is always revealed, successful or not. Every book that opens has to slam shut.

So let me tell you about the chapter my bookmark was stuck on once; so entangled, so flummoxing and so sudden that I found myself in the hospital, trying to make sense of what had just happened. There was a familiarity around the room but it was not a good one. The familiarity was of a family of hostility, dislike and blame, and the only true recognising I sensed was in my hand. I sat beside my wife's hospital bed, holding her hand; surrounded by her very concerned and tensed family.

The doctor arrived, with the MRIs and the scans. He told us that the brain injury was bad, and we could be looking at a possible coma if she wouldn't wake after a few hours. Half of her family frantically moved out, sobbing. Others went out to be with them and console each other. I sat there, beside the bed, her hand in mine. I had no one to console. I cried to her. I had no one but her.

A few hours later I felt her hand twitch, and my mind jerked up from it's tired, sleepy stance. Her breathing became heavier, and as if with a life bringing sigh, she gently and tiredly opened her eyes. My own eyes had seen no greater sight. A fresh new river of tears flowed through my eyes, as I whispered to her,

"Hey. Hey, you okay?"

She looked at me. Her eyes were the same hazel that I played hide and seek in. The depth in them when she talked was a lake I could dip myself in and drown. There was a brightness, a luminous intensity that defined her as a person. But when she looked at me, behind the hazel was an emptiness. The lights were on, but apparently, everyone had left.

I tried again. *"You-you okay?"*

She tried to speak. Coughed a little and said in a croaky voice,

"**Who are you?**"

"You were alone left out in the cold,

Clinging to the ruin of your broken home.

Too lost and hurting to carry your load,

We all need someone to hold."

Apparently, my life is one of those books where two separate stories are told to compare the tales of both - to highlight the discrepancies and contrasts, the riches and the poverty. Quite often the discrepancies are due to one's own actions in the book, and I may have made it worse than it was necessary. Upon finding myself as a foreigner in my wife's eyes, with the past wiped clean and the present rendered slight; I broke into a violent reaction that had then rendered me a 'threat to the patient'. And quite conveniently, it was a noose around my neck to keep me away from trying to get my life back. I was not allowed to see her, contact her or try to insinuate that I was, or rather am her husband, her love.

I went to our home every day, and it was still our home. She was there on the wall, in her closet, beside me on the bed, in that photo frame beside the lamp, on my laptop home screen. She was there with me, reminding me to take my pills and to wash my socks. She still yelled at me for not turning the geyser off. She still reminded me to come home soon. She was my habit, and she was with me.

I remember how she'd arch an eyebrow every time she thought I was not doing well, and ask with a gaze that was impossible to avoid. She'd look at you with her arched eyebrow and ask the same question, "All good?" To which I would always reply, "I'm okay." I was always okay, honestly, knowing that she was there, able to notice something was wrong, and asking me about it. That would solve the matters halfway as I felt I wasn't alone in any of my troubles. I used to then stand in front of our picture on the wall, alone and empty, plead into her eyes, and choke on the words,

"I'm not okay. Not. Okay."

"You've been fighting the memory all on your own,
Nothing washes, nothing grows;
I know how it feels being by yourself in the rain,
We all need someone to stay,
We all need someone to stay."

I fought. I fought with the world in the day and in the night, I came home and lost to myself. The city taunted me, reminded me of the places where we used to be 'we', and now I was only me. And yet I endured the taunts, for at every cafe, restaurant, theatre and mart I could still see her nitpicking on her sugar cubes or tomatoes, or fussing over the colour of her new dress.

I'd still go to the cafe and add exactly one and a half cube of sugar in the coffee, just how she liked it. I would order the pesto pasta at our go-to restaurant instead of my usual steak. I would go and window shop dresses, and imagine her in them, sometimes fussing at my choice of colour. "It does not go with my hair!" she'd say.

One day, as I finished my coffee, with exactly one and a half cubes of sugar, no less nor more; I saw her walking towards the cafe. I passed it off as a mirage, I was indeed imagining her everywhere. Until I saw her come to the door, pause, blink confusedly, look about, catch my eye and frown, and then slowly walk in. I sat on my table paralysed, unable to pinch myself, unable to breathe, unable to comprehend that my silent wishes have been fulfilled.

She ordered her coffee and looked for a place. Stars seemed to align again and no table was spare, except a chair in front of me. She looked in my direction and our eyes met. She slowly walked over, gracious as ever, and asked, "Excuse me, can I sit here?"

I nodded very slowly. I stared at her, took her in hungrily. My eyes didn't wet at all; for a blurry image of her, so close to me, would be a waste. Her hazel eyes now had depth, but I felt I didn't know the insides of it. Her hair was the same, luscious as ever, except she had kept it.. open. She never liked to keep her hair open on the table. Before I could notice more she moved for the sugar jar, and I instinctively said, "one and a half?"

She blinked. "Excuse me?"

I straightened myself. "Um, one and a half cubes of sugar? For your coffee?"

She smiled politely. "Ah, no, I like it a little sweet. I take two."

I smiled and passed on the jar. She picked it and added two into her cup. I watched her every movement like a star stuck child, like a teenage boy looking at his prom date. She was mixing the sugar when she looked up and asked me, " I'm sorry for just putting this here but, you don't suppose we've met before?"

I looked at her for a few seconds. Built up my courage, and said, "No, I don't think we have. Nice to meet you."

"Hear you falling and lonely, cry out,
Will you fix me up? Will you show me hope?
The end of the day, I'm helpless,
Can you keep me close? Can you love me most?"

A new chapter had turned in my book. Maybe the chain was untangling. Or maybe not. What do you call the hope of things getting better and the harsh break of the illusion, that hope is nothing but a torture method? I think it is called reality.

And yet, she still hated late night outs. She was still very environmentally conscious. She was still extremely punctual. She still had the same caring air about her. She still wanted to be on the good books of everyone she met. And within there, she was still the woman I loved.

I remember how I proposed to her. It was a solemn, peaceful evening atop of a hill, and I had asked her to say out the five people she'd never want to lose. The catch was, she also had to mention what would be the best gift for them. And as expected, I came the last, and she said she would gift me a ring. Her perceptive qualities ruined the surprise, but it was a fun proposal. Hints of that perception, the ability to read people, to scan ***me*** was still there. My love was still in there somewhere.

"You've drunk it down and now you've spat it out,
Nothing tastes like the things you had,
So tear it off, why don't you let them go?
We all need someone to stay,
We all need someone to stay."

My life was healthy. I started eating steak with her. One and a half cubes of sugar had risen up to two. My book was at the climax stage where I was anxious to take a peek at the final pages to see how everything unfolds. Alas, there was no way to do that.

Her family contacted me, and warned me about trying to make her remember her past. Little did they know that the memories of our past were just a benchmark, one I had broken it multiple times already. It was the memories I was making with her that mattered the most - a new sprout out of a fallen tree.

Torn between our conjoined past and our yo-yoing present, I needed to know where to be, what to do and how to feel. Torn, conflicted, I needed to ask if what I was doing was correct. I needed to know if my story of re-finding love ends this chapter or not. Sunken face and darkened eyes became my look, and one fine day, while eating a steak, I could feel her gaze on me.

I looked up, and she had her arms crossed, eyebrow raised. "All okay?" She asked.

I grinned. "All good," I replied. "All good."

"You can still see where the water was,
In a line at the top of the chimney bricks,

Sometimes, something so broken can never be fixed.

So we saved a few things that were spared,

And brought it to the ground,

Cause you always build it better the second time around."

It was time. I had found love again. No, it wasn't the same woman. No, it wasn't the same love. It was something more. Something new. Something better. I believed I had done all the effort to make her fall in love with me again, and yet, she fell in love with a different me and I fell in a different love with her, again. She was not my wife anymore, but I sure wanted to make her my wife again.

So I took her to the sea. I asked her to say out the five people she'd never want to lose. The catch was, she also had to mention what would be the best gift for them. And this time, I came the first, and she said she would gift me a ring; and put in my palm our old wedding ring.

"I'm sleeping more and eating again,

I'm starting over like a factory town,

And you always build it better the second time around,

You always build it better the second time around,

You always build it better the second time around."

Quote lyrics from 'Someone To Stay - Vancouver Sleep Clinic' and 'Build It Better - Aron Wright'.

You reap what you repress.

Halfway To Asphodel.com

LETTERS TO CELISEN

Letter To Celisen #1

Dear C;

I write to you today amidst the chaos of a transition. As you very well know, transitions are noisy and crude, so I'm sure you aren't surprised I haven't been able to write much to you. As it is, we are together on the white only for a short while this time.

It's the night, the world is quiet and I feel your presence. The cool breeze pulls me towards the bed but I feel your consciousness. I know I wouldn't be able to sleep even if I did hit the bed.

Things seem to have settled down in my life, which I feel is the calm before another storm. You did, however, change your tune in the last letter, which I feel you have a right to. It did still surprise me, realising someone as wise and mature like you also can have a change of mind. It was probably unfair on my part to not expect that or to imagine you as infallible, but still, I found myself questioning all I had done and learnt.

I have no reason to worry, though as I remodelled my approach based on your previous guidelines (tweaking them a little, but I'm sure you understand) and things settled down well. Not completely, but enough for me to revel in your sagacity again.

What does one do when all one has learnt stands nullified? Or when one's cocoon of knowingness is torn apart? The feeling of uselessness that follows is a rather uncomfortable one. It sure seems to be a problem which I'll encounter in greater capacity later on so I will bombard you with its details later, provided I still have your permission to take a dip into your lake of knowledge.

That lake of yours is a funny thing. Some may drown in it, as I intend to; while some may only splash some of its waters on them. Many don't even play with its waters, creating ripples and waves but some have the droplets splashed onto them by others. Despite that, the fact that people do find your lake is something remarkable. It gives me a hint that you may actually be omnipresent. If that's so, do I still need to write you letters?

Nevertheless, as I embark upon a new journey, I may settle in different environments. While I still believe I will have your company there as well, although I will have to find a different quirk to reach out to you. There may be times when I fail, but see, even my lack of reply is a message in itself. And I'll take your lack of reply as an indication of you telling me to 'do it yourself.'

I think I am now finding it easier to reach out to you, and feel like the frequency of our exchanges is increasing. In the case of me not being able to write to you, I hope you'll seek me out. But rest assured, I will find you, now I know that it's easier deep into the night.

Sleep may not be beckoning me tonight, but the body is still weary for rest.

The nomad who knows only how to find you;

Funadrius.

LETTER TO CELISEN #2

Dear C;

Over the past few weeks, I haven't heard from you. I'm sure that is a reason for each of our well being, which points to neither of us actually having the need to call upon each other. I actually find it rather relaxing that the only way to reach out to you is by the old fashioned letter written in solitude, in spite of the hundreds of other ways available at our disposal to impede the sanctity of one's time.

I write to you today not because I am devoid of anything worthwhile to do, I write because I have a lot on my hands but nothing on my mind. Things have spiralled downwards into a point where my focus is calm, surrounded by a whirlwind of other matters. And when I'm calm, I am reminded of you.

It's pretty evident from our exchanges that I need you more ever than you need me, and despite anything going on in your life you always seem to manage a few words for me. That inexplicably is probably the best thing anyone has ever done for me, and as I've shared before, the fact that neither of us needs each other's pings regularly seems to keep what we have sacred.

I have been pretty conflicted about what is going to come and how do I prepare myself for it, as you very well know. Every night I look to share my worries to you but never managed to jot it all down, maybe I needed a larger than usual piece of quietly disquiet to finally pick up the pen. Have you ever been in a situation where your clutch achievement is in sight, your destined journey about to begin, and you stand on your doorstep wondering whether all your past penance and future forethought remains valid? I feel like Bilbo Baggins at 50.

The past seems irrelevant, even though I cannot possibly forget it's role in the development I have had. The future seems insurmountable, though it may be an illusion. It would be rather unfair to say I'm torn physically, but mentally it sure is stretching away on my core.

However difficult it may seem, I need your voice. I know that gnawing away my days and nights will offer no solution, but as we all know it, we humans are more prone to worry rather than freedom - we look out for agony like the sea reaches out for the shore.

I apologize for going on about my own state, for you must have your own things going on. I don't think I can ever put in words my gratitude I have for you. And if ever do you need (not that I ever think you will) a drop of my thoughts for your ocean of wisdom, you know where to find me.

I suppose you do not have much time, and I could write away until dawn.

I am, and always will be, waiting for your voice and words.

Yours,

Funadrius

Letter To Celisen #3

C;

The evening breeze sweeps in via the window, disturbing the wind chimes on its way; the setting sun bathes my study in orange and the sky in red; as I finally pick up the parchment to write to you.

The last letter I sent you contained a huge part of my problems to wreck your time, and I have spent the time until your reply as if I have dumped them onto you. Somewhere, however, in the back of my mind, I knew that you would reply and that on that day, I would have to face something more than the problems I sent your way. You, of course, have your time to avenge.

Your reply, of course, primarily reinstated the notion that you're well, and your words assured me as much. I wonder if I caught you off guard with my letter, and whether you were discomfited, and if that was the case, I apologise profusely. I know you have a few windows where you can be reached out to, and how easily you get disturbed with the slightest of bother.

Your reply to my last letter came as a calm respite to the turmoil I asked you to fish me out of, but it also brought with it a fair amount of new questions and thought-provoking dilemmas. The more I seek a solution from you, things either escalate for the worse or I stare into the face of two more problems. Nevertheless, you have never denied me any guidance and nor have you refuted any attempt of mine; so I will remain grateful and continue to disturb you.

Your solution to what seemed to be a very complex scenario turned out to be equally simple. I find it really exasperating as to how sometimes the most complex of tangles can be straightened by pulling a single thread, but we instead make the many knots tighter by pulling the wrong threads. As you stated, it is crucial to evaluate the scenario in full detail before trying to resolve it, as the simplest way is often beneath a thin veil right in front of you. In a way, it reminds me of you, as I have to shun away the curtains of my monotone to encounter you and your wisdom.

Enacting upon your easy solution may be the most difficult task I've ever faced, and it may soon pose a paradoxical scenario of a bad deed, an evil mission and a righteous fight. As I step into the wilderness armed with my will and your wisdom, I hope to make people see the difference.

I hope people see the difference between someone who's done a bad deed and someone who are evil, because, as unfortunate as it is, bad exists in each of us, so does evil in the society.

One way I thought it would work was to introduce as many as I could to you, but that would not only be impractical but also hypocritical on my side, as that would mean a complete disrespect of what we have.

The world needs more of you, S. I need more of you.

I remain your protege and your student;

Yours;

Funadrius.

Letter To Celisen #4

C;

It has been ages since we last exchanged words. Time has flown by, and with each passing day, I have felt your waning influence on my life. The chaos and pandemonium that had engulfed me seemed to increase by the Fibonacci, and I could either have waited for peace after being deaf or actively seek you out.

It's not that I've haven't considered the former option, but in the recent days, the commotion became so huge that I was left with no other option than to knock on your shoulder again. I know it's terribly selfish to do so, but let me tell you, it was an attempt to not be self-centred when I refrained from contacting you all this time. Trust me, it feels quite egocentric, and to an extent, even narcissistic to keep on hounding you at any slight inconvenience that befalls on me. But you, being you, have never ever told me off or showed any signs of resentment; providing wholesome guidance along the way. It makes me further revel in your ageless acumen.

Speaking of age, why do we take age as a barometer for prudence and competency? And why does a higher number is taken to be hierarchically superior? Surely it has to be about the experiences that define a man? I accept that generally, a long-lived life has a greater scope of accumulating experiences, but that does not state a written down fact that every forty years old is wiser than a twenty-year-old! Forgive me for my lack of humility, but I believe I'm more sagacious than a fair few people elder than me.

There is, however, a certain know how that does only come with age. And again, I bear testament to that, acknowledging that there were some puzzles and constrictions years ago that resolved on their own as my age increased and vision expanded; without having the loud need to seek desperate answers. Even as yet, I tend to believe - again a little a haughtily - that such epiphanies happen to everyone at a certain point of age, so it is more of a ladder of revelations everyone climbs rather than choosing plush berries of involvement from a thorny bush.

I am back to my old hunting ground, away from the transitions I mentioned last time out. Somehow I find it easier to locate you here, as it has become a thing of habit. I do need to find out new ways to experience you at different locations.

But yes, it doesn't mean you cannot find me yourself. I know you stated subtly that you locating people doesn't usually spell out a fortune for them, but you're still welcome at my doorstep.

A lover who doesn't know what he loves;

Funadrius.

Letter To Celisen #5

C;

I seem to be lost in a maze, a maze whose walls are as high as the sky and whose floor is filled with slime. Even if I wish to, I cannot stop navigating, but that's no problem as I don't wish to stop. I seem to be looking for something, and I am not specifically sure what it is. Furthermore, I am not even sure whether that something is at the centre of the maze or outside it.

To you, then, my conquest may seem very pointless, but it makes sense to me. Yet I don't know how, but I keep on moving, unwilling to halt. You see, I am like a whirlwind of leaves, moving around. If I stop, I will disperse, disintegrate and die.

Within this turmoil, I try to invoke you once again, from impossible reaches and uncharted positions. For once, or maybe once again, I am not sure whether this letter will find it's mark, or whether I will ever be able to embrace your witticisms again. The cloth of my past which I have been trying to iron remains crumpled, while I am entwined with stitching the present and worrying about the unstitched cloth of the future.

I am on a large endeavour, as I have told you, one which I do not know how successful it will be, but I am nevertheless determined to finish it off. Sometimes the acceptance doesn't matter as much as the fulfilling of a dream, as a dream fulfilled is equal to growing higher in our own eyes.

However, as much as well objected my quest seems, I have problems. Walking along on pathways I seem to be trudging the same path over and over again, irrespective of how different I try to be. What seems to be the problem, I know not. It's like I keep on taking the same turns - the right is left and what's left is right. And going back is not an option.

Do I need something else? Something extra? Something from within? I feel like I am water choosing to flow on the path already wet; until and unless the gush is too forceful, in which case it barrages through and creates its own path.

In your response, you questioned the source of my newfound wisdom, and I'm rather offended as to why you'd think there would be any other source except you. Sure there are sources apart from you, but you know I don't treasure them as much. Now you would go on to say that I should explore them, which I am, but none have the pull that you possess.

I'm sorry if this letter comes across to you as an incoherent rant, which is what it exactly is, but I felt like I needed to vent these out. It's a little ingloriously insolent of me to treat you as a 'dump yard', but it is your magnanimous grace which allows me this liberty.

Having 'dumped' things onto you;

Your forlorn friend;

Funadrius.

The Last Letter To Celisen

C;

Let's just say, people know about you and me. And that might just be my fault.

I am not sure if an apology suffices, but within the narrow boundaries of meagre things I can provide you, it the best which I can offer now. Your angry quiet is very plausibly vindicated, and it's fitting that even you reach out to yourself, for introspection is to the soul what water is to thirst.

Your reticence led to voids in my nights. There were gaps wherein I could not do, see hear or think anything. As you know, I've been there before, but back then you were the escape, and now you were the cause. Despite that, these voids weren't troubling as many.

You see, things have changed. Times have changed. And probably, I've changed as well. As someone who forays into the wilderness out of choice rather than curiosity, I found myself stuck in a vivid maze of machines and bricks – an utterly new dimension of wilderness. Although I am not very certain that I've changed perceptively, I leave the deceptive chalice of perception at your lips, as you've earned the right to judge me as harshly as you want to.

As I said, I am in an altogether new level of wilderness, some things have remained the same. The rain is still with me, and it refuses to be quiet at times, much to my (your?) fury. Rains, I've found, are like good poetry. You can only enjoy the rain when you're completely immersed in it or when you hear it in peace –

something I have been able to do recently. I genuinely feel that people who appreciate rains also appreciate the subtler things in life. Night rains are a different beast altogether. They resemble the subconscious that roars and drops while you're asleep.

People who love the night rains are generally on the road to self-awareness, I feel.

Beyond that, there's a notable dissonance between my heart and my mind.

My heart beats differently here. It's very.. *happy*. And it isn't used to it. Just like an 11-year-old Harry Potter was confused about being told that he was a wizard, my heart is befuddled about being happy. It is joyous and chirpy, while also being anxious and wary of this entire episode being a sham. And the nags of anxiousness come from my ever skeptical mind - which is not its fault either. My mind is the centre of logic, and logic doesn't accept anything which defies trends.

As you know, I've been fighting the dark for a while, and slowly it has become my comfort zone. Now, I've been ushered into the light, and it is scaring me. Not because I'm pushed into something different, but because the I'm so used to the dark I'm scared that the light may hurt me or blind me. I may be darkness' step-son, and I'm afraid of the unacceptance of light.

Let's put it this way; I'm not afraid of the light as a vampire is. I'm anxious about it as Batman is, cause without the night, both him and I are nothing.

I need to adjust to good now. I need to adjust to some acceptance, and I need to adjust to belongingness. I need to balance the hands on my shoulders and the hugs. I need to adjust to being happy.

Am I being too whiny? Are my questions valid?

Anyway, glad to finally reach out to you again. I'm sorry, I am terrible at apologizing and reconcillation.

Your stargazing apprentice;

Funadrius.

POETRY

That, Mi Amigo, Is Love

There's life in talking,
and there's talking to life.
when that coincides,
that, mi amigo, is love.

When your words touch and move on,
When your touch inspires someone's words,
that, mi amigo, is love.

When the shoulders that keep your head,
lend another support,
that, mi amigo, is love.

When the music that you feel,
conveys your essence to someone,
that, mi amigo, is love.

When the rain brings the petrichor,
and the petrichor brings her,
that, mi amigo, is love.

When the moments new,
bring back the ghosts of moments dead,
that, mi amigo, is love.

And when you realise it's all of you,
with all of her,

always within you,
that, mi amigo, is when you finally realise it's love.

A Tryst With Trust

A string of letters, the yarn of words;
Truths and lies and sayings of sorts.
Knitting together a tapestry of swords;
Feeling and fueling the flames of hordes.

The sea was selfish, he could have sworn;
Doesn't let you swim with the crown.
But as shortly as you're dead and forlorn;
Nor even will it let you drown.

Loaded with loads and loads of loads;
With the weight threatening to disembody.
For the dead man in the dead sea showed;
The weight was life, not the body.

If faith can move mountains, say oh lord!
Why tempt, build and mould evil?
Afraid about who will pray to you, god;
If there was no devil?

The lone traveler of the fading night;
Prepares to say adieu in the morning.
For what he tried to say with all his might;
Was all to be mistaken as mourning.

Falling and stumbling, he is done;
Charred and burnt and ripe with thirst.
'Cause life plays a fiery game with some;
For they've made a tryst with trust.

Assumptions

She told me she was busy,
and the wait made me queasy.
But she wouldn't come and talk,
I knew I couldn't just balk.

She said I'll fill you in,
Said she's never been busy akin.
But I needed to speak,
Hence the approach I had to tweak.

I needed words certain,
Honest, barring any curtain.
Her absence asked me questions,
Tearing apart my close substance.

There were gaps I needed to fill,
But then she took seemingly ill.
I filled the gaps with deductions,
Which aptly aided my functions.

Things became normal,
Nothing remained formal.
I let loose a deduction,
Was astounded by her reaction.

She balked, she sulked,
Unimpressed with the stories I sculpt,
Finally explaining under complusion,
Said I made a lot many assumptions.

Pieces Of Me

Dim stars and a dark moon;
Whence the grief stands tall;
And the night end's nowhere soon;
I'll be there to pick up your call.

As the night gets colder;
And you can't give your best;
I'll lend you my shoulder;
And let your head rest.

When the going gets tough;
And sleep deserts your bed;
Knock on my door enough;
I'll take your worry instead.

Your love, your life and time;
Caress them with a smile;
Believe these words of mine;
That It'll be okay after a while.

But when my night turns dark;
And it becomes colder;
I hope you remember my mark;
And we will recall times older.

I give pieces of me to heal you with;
Do keep those pieces with you;
And so when I'm really hit;
I hope you bring them with you.

Roads Diverged In The Wood (Poem)

Many roads diverged in the yellow wood,
Shall he take the weathered one, as the mellow would?
Or burst behind the mob, as the callow would?
Cautious and dwelling, the fellow stood.

The crossroad conundrum, a decision in the null,
The question daunting, enthralling a savage pull,
Ere Janus stands, his mystic advice in full,
To marshal or mimic, but not shun in a lull.

A tale of uncommon, the affable chap,
Hoping of naught more than a thunderous clap.
The ordinary call, the trod regularly recap,
Or to fray a novel course, and build a gap?

A crafty scheme of two, destiny and destination,
The lad must brood to make up a decision.
To choose either, maybe dodge the stipulation
To outwit a god, much to his consternation.

The heart beats left, the mind whispers right,
He listens to whom, bows to whose might?
Knows not the future, the Holy Grail in sight,
Dares to take a step, and fall in the fight?

He plays the game and wins the mete,
Picks his destination and uses the fate.
Moves a step ahead, loosens an unsolved strait.
Marches on steadily, there's nothing to haste.

Forget You, I Will

Forget you I will;
If you can ever forgive me.

Forget your habits I will;
If you can stop looking for me on the bed every morning.

Forget your gifts I will;
If you can ever quantify us in things.

Forget the ecstasy I will;
When you stop instinctively looking for my hug.

Forget your talks I will;
When you can look at the sky and not wish me beside.

Forget our walks I will;
If you find a shoulder as comfortable as mine.

Forget my hoodie I will;
If you can ignore my warmth when you wear it.

Forget my pain I will;
When you have as many sleepless nights as me.

Forget your memories I will;
If you could ever remember all the dandelions we picked.

Forget our time I will;
If you can tear our picture exactly in half.

Forget your scent I will;
If you can ever forget the feel of my nuzzle on your neck.

Forget your touch I will;
If you can let anyone else touch you.

Forget it all I will;
If you can forget the taste of my lips.

Forget your love I will;
If you can remove me from your past.

Forget you I will;
If you can ever forget me back.

A Broken Melancholy

A single sheet, within it I sheathe;
Worn on a side, undisturbed on the other.
Warm on one side, cold on the other,
The difference making me seethe.

The unseeable border, like a wall of glass;
Like waters of seas that do not mix,
Impenetrable, impermeable, yet strong as bricks,
Containing me, while it outlasts me, alas!

The shadows on the moonlit wall dance;
A petrifying tale of scarcity, gain and loss.
The outlines grow bold, detach and come across,
Catching my chest with teeth, nail and a lance.

A hysterical bellow, and on she turns the light;
Tearing past the silhouttes and the demon,
Embraces me, and leaves me a freeman,
Brings me to senses, and leaves me benight.

I wept into a frenzy, into my part of the sheet;
As I tolerate a brimful dearth of love,
For mine is selfish, needy of the beloved,
And she left, liberated from me as a feat.

A proud and egotistic love, the one I harbour tod;
Seeking it's one definite other half,
Maybe a love so selfless, be her epitaph,
Is it there or is it not, oh God?

Answer me, O presupposed divine;
Where, when and how does end my drought?
Where to see, hear, search and shout,
Act, show, speak, and rejoinder my whine.

Alas, the God I know is a handicapped one,
If he's all seeing, then he's definitely earless.
If he's all listening then he's formless.
And if he's all doing, then naturally he's eyeless.
And finally, if he's all knowing, then his voice is none.

Do You?

Do you remember;
The nights and the skies,
The love and it's disguise,
Our tunes and reprise,
The clouds we made from sighs?

Do you remember;
The lows and the highs,
Our clasped hands on thighs,
And if you can ever surmise,
my loneliness through your eyes?

Do you understand;
'Our' demise,
Wrapped in a miragelike guise,
Which smilingly implies,
The impeding goodbyes?

Do you wish to know;
Which cryptic surmise,
Does the truth actually belies,
And when does arise,
Our collective chastise?

Do you want to say;
A farewell which decries,
An affinity which it defies,
Wherein we both despise,
The whats, hows and the whys?

She Loves Me

She indulges me;
Like the sea it's shore,
And like a child I ask more.

She suffers me;
Like a widow her pain,
Unbearable, but there to stay.

She feels me;
Like a bird feels the sky,
Fully, and truly thereby.

She influences me;
Like a teacher her student,
Disregard her I wouldn't.

She embraces me;
Like a parent their child,
Strong, but also mild.

She touches me;
Like the sun touches the dew,
A touch felt by very few.

She knows me;
Like a friend knows another,
As closely as a brother.

She likes me;
As the trees the breeze,
Evident, but still disagrees.

She eyes me;
Like the loved their betrothed,
Forever till the end of the road.

She loves me;
Like the moon the stars,
Every night, despite her scars.

To Roads Diverged In The Yellow Wood

To roads diverged in the yellow wood;
Why do you tear me so?
Making me choose between could and should;
Knowing I'll have to reap what I sow.

They say both have a unique charm;
And I am free to choose any.
Then I ponder about what harm;
Does my decision do to many?

One is weathered and the other fresh;
The choice would be an obvious one.
Unless and until I make a mess;
And go about paving a new one?

I look back and see eyes of stone;
Which gaze into the distance far ahead.
Meeting them chills me to my bone;
Yet I carry on treading ahead.

Cutting through the rocks and gravel;
I pave my way with insistence.
Thus made a new road to travel;
And that has made all the difference.

ARTHUR, ARTHUR

Arthur, Arthur in the phone;
Who's the craziest in the unknown?
When the world preys and prays,
Who's the one cast and thrown?

Arthur, Arthur in the phone;
Who's the loner most prone?
Coming home to be a lone,
Who's the bad man cast in stone?

Arthur, Arthur in the phone;
Whose screams are sung intone?
You give, give and only give,
Whats truly your own?

Arthur, Arthur in the phone;
Whose life do you disown?
All your flaws flayed to the bone
All else's to condone.

Arthur, Arthur in the phone;
What do you know unbeknown?
All your life and all your cents,
And one shall be your clone.

Arthur, Arthur, in the phone;
Why do you lay and groan?
Laugh, and put up a happy face,
Cause you, you are not alone.

THE MILLION PLUS ONE'TH WHEEL.

The door opens and closes,
And no one meets my eye.
And some with their purposes,
Struggle to say a hi.

I had made new friends,
Was one among the three.
But pavements are broad for only two,
And so I let them be.

I then got into a quartet,
And was happy to belong,
But the auto-rickshaw takes in a triplet,
And so I walked all along.

A group of four took me in,
But it became one too many.
one can listen to three at best.
So I threw in my penny.

And every night do I bemoan,
Thinking this is how it is to be life long.
Within people, yet all alone,
A part, but still don't belong.

No matter what vehicle I join,
I'll always be the extra wheel.
In the world of a million,
The million plus one'th wheel.

On Fire

My soul is on fire,
Blazing, untamed yet restrained.
It escapes in my fury,
Vents and risings.

Rebellions and flaring,
Have become synonymous with;
Scorching breaths of words,
Crude and melting.

My insides are on fire,
As it chars the body black.
Black from within, you are;
Is all what they can say.

Now all I sense is a burn
Within, and I'm told it's
The stomach acid, then
why do I breathe out smoke?

Turns out Pompeii,
Is all within me,
With masterful sculptures of death;
With a shining ember.

And that ember, still
Glowing bright; and
Nothing can douse,
My heart that's on fire.

Cemented

The night pours its dark ink,
Onto the blank canvas of my day,
Peace scampers in a blink,
As I gaze through the grey.

I fear the past aghast,
And wish for a pleasant present.
Yet the future approaches fast,
As I stand stuck in cement.

It isn't a night, they say;
It is but just a tunnel.
However dark be it may,
There's an end to the null.

Yet every ray of light I saw,
With my eyes at a strain,
I prepared myself for a maul,
As it was sure to be a train.

Never did come the mauling,
Nor did arrive the respite.
All I could hear was howling,
I wasn't alone in my plight.

The cement became quicksand,
And I seep beneath the surface.
Desperation drives my hand,
As I struggle to save my face.

My hand finds someone's,
A despairing, desperate meet,
Alas, it was too little too late,
And slowly succumbs my heartbeat.

Purgatory asks me how I was,
As they weigh my sins.
But they never accounted for my loss,
Neither did they care about my wins.

They told me I can choose,
Between redemption and pain,
And I chose to pay my dues,
Only to stand in the cement again.

How It Is Like..

They asked me,
What is it like
To be so afraid of betrayal,
That you push everyone away?

What is it like,
To be so afraid of not fitting in,
That you instigate your desolation?

What is it like,
To be so afraid of rejection,
That you stop trying?

What is it like,
To be so afraid of heartbreak,
That you begin fearing love?

And I told them;
How it is like,
To know true loyalty,
That you don't let many in.

How it is like,
To be so fond of the right belonging,
That you aren't truly lonely.

How it is like,
To know true acceptance,
That you just be you.

How it is like,
To have felt a love,
Which cannot be replaced or repeated.

Inner Hounds

My night is a friend of the slinky moon,
Which hides behind the dark clouds.
Warm summer winds caress my face,
As I stand trapped in the concrete canopy.

The residual peace is unmatched within,
As a savage storm brews in my guts,
My conscience threatens to rip apart,
Like huts ravaged by Poseidon's wrath.

Behind me I hear dark growls;
And I turn to see fiery, red eyes.
The hounds have found me at last,
***Fear**, **Pain**, **Hate**, and **Envy** on my trails.*

Fighting them was my one soul purpose;
Which I bravely let forego eons ago.
They've been chasing my smell since,
For destroying me is their sole purpose.

If I run I survive, if I stop I perish;
The hounds' hunger heighting me hell.
But tonight they have me cornered,
Outnumbered, outsized, out-thought.

***Fear** looks hungrily at my guts,*
Drool dripping down his fangs.
***Pain** measures me up patiently,*
Checking if I still have some fight in.

***Hate** is restless, wants to eat me alive;*
Yipping and snarling at my every move.
***Envy** blocks my escape routes,*
Essentially trapping me and my fate.

Yet they won't attack, much to my surprise;
As if they're awaiting an order.
As if there's more to this pack,
A leader, most ferocious, I realise.

A new, loud howl pierces the din,
as a new yet familiar beast enters the fray.
Larger, bulkier and hungrier than any;
*The **Wounded Pride** enters the melee.*

This is it, then, in a wild night;
Me fighting my inner direwolves.
This is how it ends, I thought;
Gnawed and eaten by dire wolves.

*First, **Fear** snaps away at my guts,*
***Pain** lunges for my throbbing heart.*
***Hate** tears away my long gone head,*
*as **Envy** like always, holds me back.*

*But **Wounded Pride** will not join in,*
For it is not his job to kill.
His job was to sire the four cubs,
*Via his beastly ways with **Lust**.*

Conquered me, finally, they have;

Ripped by ***Fear, Pain, Hate*** *and* ***Envy****.*
Yet, keenly finished by ***Wounded Pride****,*
But truly killed by an insatiable ***Lust****.*

TRUDGE ON, TRUDGE ON

When the clock ticks silently;
And rest has left, all abandon;
Take a few steps, breathe quietly;
And trudge on, trudge on, into the horizon.

When presence is a mist;
And thus walks in aberration;
Stand and remember the gist;
And trudge on, trudge on, into the horizon.

When your shoulder has a chip;
And pleas are met with accusation;
Well your eyes and seal your lip;
And trudge on, trudge on, into the horizon.

When your arms are out;
And warmth is just an allusion;
Remind yourself that it's okay to shout;
And trudge on, trudge on, into the horizon.

The world is dark and it is difficult to see;
But do not give in to aversion;
Understand that you have a place to be;
And trudge on, trudge on, into the horizon.

What Am I?

What is my past,
If not an
Immensely heavy anchor?

What is my present,
If not the
Struggle to stay afloat?

What is my future,
If not the
Quest to Ogygia?

What is pain,
If not the
Tipsiness of ignorance?

What is hurt,
If not the
Lines I write?

What are tears,
If not the
Leftovers of you?

What is the night,
If not the
Winds of solitude?

What is the day,

If not the
Escape from the night?

What is liberation,
If not the
Songs I sing?

What is love,
If not the
Tapering of cracks?

What is happiness,
If not the
Resemblance in art?

What is life,
If not the
Gradual healing?

What am I,
If not
All I am?

Vivre En Moi

If you heard me out,
You'd know of people new
The naysayers,
The ear buzzers
The liars and their squires.

If you saw me through,
You'd see the pain anew
The weeping heart,
The oozing soul
The tired act of my mind mired.

If you talked to me soon,
You'd know of pain accrued
The nightly gaze,
The daily faze,
The steps of daze and cliches.

But if you lived with me true,
And didn't bid me adieu,
You'd know of my ability to reveal,
To feel, conceal and heal,
Truly with all my will and zeal.

Tears

Tears, warm tears,
Flow by my side.
Scaling the skin
Very much alive,
A remnant of what's died.

Tears, unwanted tears,
Flow by my side.
Tickling the cheek,
Which betray
A message's bespeak.

Tears, sad tears,
Flow by my side.
Drawing a sniff,
Drawing attention,
But it's no one's tiff.

Tears, happy tears,
Flow by my side.
Making a funny sight,
Never seen before,
Hidden behind might.

Tears, healing tears,
Flow by my side.
Wash the eyes,
Clearing my vision,
As the trail dries.

Tears, loving tears,
Flow by my side.
They're not to wipe,
as they're the proof,
Of someone's gripe.

Consist

She listens to me
Even if I've nothing to say.
And she sees things in me,
When I have nothing to show.
She stays with me,
When I have nothing to give,
She stands by me,
When I'm struggling to live.
She talks to me,
Even if I can't see her above.
She comes back to me,
When I'm struggling to love.

I Swear I Loved

In my dreams of fear,
And in days that near,
Within my nights of solitude,
Beyond the reaches of my fortitude,
Shatters my heart.
And with every broken shard,
I swear I loved.

From memories of hands grasped,
To the empty handed truth,
Far away from my clutches of reality,
I reminiscise with wistful brutality,
Which cracks open my heart.
And with every broken shard,
I swear I loved.

Between those who don't do for me,
And those who do "for me",
Away from the masks which say the truth,
Near those faces which lie,
Bursts my heart.
And with every broken shard,
I swear I loved.

Yet with every rise of dawn,
After every fall of dusk,
Each piece throbs a little faster,
Even though its been through disaster,
Beats my heart.

And with every broken shard,
I swear I loved.

YOU OWE ME

Let it be known,
That you're with no thing.
Let it be told,
That you owe me nothing.

But let me tell you,
That you sowed in me something.
Let me tell you,
That you owe me something.

You owe me the hours,
That I spent with chagrin
You owe me the flowers,
That I placed within.

You owe me the worries,
That I devoted to you,
You owe me the stories,
That I so willingly told you.

You owe me my breaths,
Which I let go as sighs.
You owe me the deaths,
That I died in disguise.

You owe me the walks,
That I travelled with you.
You owe me the talks,
That I shared with you.

You owe me the sleep,
Which never returned to me,
You owe me the weep,
Which now burns in me.

You owe me the nights,
That I stayed awake for.
You owe me the lights,
And who I lit them for.

Rocks and Fire

I thoroughly believe the mire,
That the moon and the stars are lies.
They are nothing but rocks and fire,
Pretty from afar, set only to agonize.

So I won't promise you the literal moon,
Or the talk of 'from the moon and back'.
I won't wish for you to the stars,
They are probably dead within the black.

Yet I hope to be the rocky moon,
Driving waves to you at your behest.
And I pray to be the starry fire,
Burning within your eyes and chest.

End.

WHAT THEY SAID

Read what the everyday readers have to say..

From closet bookworms, to writers, and teachers alike; see how they judged "The Best of Halfway To Asphodel: 2015-2017"!

"Halfway To Asphodel" came out of nowhere and completely engulfed me with emotions. If only I was as talented as Vishvaraj, I could explain what I mean by that here. It's kinda hard to believe that this is his first book because the maturity shown by Vishvaraj is way beyond his age. If you're gonna read one book in 2018, make sure it's this."

- Prithvi Raj

"This collection is about maturity. The best thing is that it has potential to influence a person of any age. Vishvaraj makes many readers relate to his musings. To each reader the meaning of these texts will be different individually, but it will always leave a positive impact on their mind."

- Bhavya Makhania; Reader, Photographer, and Engineer.

"First of all, the title of the book is intriguing and made me pick up the book. And I am delighted to have read this book. The author wants to talk to the world, instead of talking… he chose to write. The book is deep and well-written. There are 5 parts in the book. I loved the authors contemplative philosophies and poems.

Loved this line: "Imagination – it grips you, sucking you in like a black hole. A pleasurable black hole, because you control that simulation."

You will find quotes from different authors throughout the book. If you love poem, then this book is for you. The personal experiences and deep thoughts of the author is visionary.

The book spreads positivity, happiness and love. I personally feel one can reread the book innumerable times.

A must read. Recommended to all. "

- Beulah Jenifer

"The way he presented the book and the language this book is written is wonderful. The simple, crisp and interesting language which one can easily connect with. The author's maturity is truly depicted in his writing style."

- Vidhya Thakkar

"I must say that he has a gift of presenting the deepest of emotions and thoughts in ink. I have, many a times, been mesmerised by his vocabulary and choice of words at the right time."

- Angad Kohli; Reader, Explorer.

"To sum up everything, I would say that The Best of Halfway to Asphodel is a compilation of the different philosophies, thoughts of the author, his experiences, the lessons he had been taught by life and most of all, his perception of life. He has a very good grip of language and it is evident in his word play. The narration throughout the book is very smooth and he has given words to his thoughts and had been successful in putting it to paper."

- Bookarlo

"He is one of those writers who pays attention to the smallest details and that's exactly what I love about his work. Once you start to read, you cannot stop. It's that intriguing. What he writes make you think."

- Dhwani Shah; Instagram Blogger (@dhw_ani)

"The author has taken his own experiences and interpretations, his perception of life, and carved magic in these 200-something pages. The language is flowy and, at several places, the author has managed to very aptly quote contemporary writings, making his experiences very relatable. (This book was a much needed breather from the shoddily edited books that are coming out a dozen a day.)"

- Mishika Singh

Elpis in a Jar is out!

"Elpis in a Jar decodes the little things in life which are often overlooked or swept under the carpet. The book takes into consideration the power of words in small groups; joining together to form poetry and texts which have hit the author between his monotone. Elpis in a Jar is a book for anyone who contemplates in their spare time and ponders over mundane things for their beauty, charm and value. This book is the second book of the author Vishvaraj Chauhan - a self-taught writer and blogger."

www.ingramcontent.com/pod-product-compliance
Ingram Content Group UK Ltd.
Pitfield, Milton Keynes, MK11 3LW, UK
UKHW021404190726
13845UKWH00028B/877

9 789354 076060